Common Sense Economics

Third Edition

Common Sense Economics

*What Everyone Should Know
About Wealth and Prosperity*

JAMES D. GWARTNEY

FLORIDA STATE UNIVERSITY

RICHARD L. STROUP

NORTH CAROLINA STATE UNIVERSITY

DWIGHT R. LEE

SOUTHERN METHODIST UNIVERSITY

TAWNI H. FERRARINI

NORTHERN MICHIGAN UNIVERSITY

JOSEPH P. CALHOUN

FLORIDA STATE UNIVERSITY

ST. MARTIN'S PRESS NEW YORK

Dedicated to our students,
past, present, and future

COMMON SENSE ECONOMICS: THIRD EDITION. Copyright © 2005, 2010, 2016 by
James D. Gwartney, Richard L. Stroup, Dwight R. Lee, Tawni H. Ferrarini, and
Joseph P. Calhoun. All rights reserved. Printed in the United States of America.
For information, address St. Martin's Press, 175 Fifth Avenue, New York, N.Y.
10010.

www.stmartins.com

Library of Congress Cataloging-in-Publication Data)

Names: Gwartney, James D., author.
Title: Common sense economics : what everyone should know about wealth and
    prosperity / James D. Gwartney, Florida State University, Richard L. Stroup, North
    Carolina State University, Dwight R. Lee, Southern Methodist University, Tawni H.
    Ferrarini, Northern Michigan University, Joseph P. Calhoun, Florida State University.
Description: Third edition. | New York : St. Martin's Press, [2016] | Includes index.
Identifiers: LCCN 2016003179| ISBN 9781250106940 (hardcover) |
    ISBN 9781250106957 (e-book)
Subjects: LCSH: Free enterprise. | Wealth. | Economics. | Finance, Personal. | Saving
    and investment.
Classification: LCC HB95 .G9 2016 | DDC 330—dc23
LC record available at http://lccn.loc.gov/2016003179

Our books may be purchased in bulk for promotional, educational, or business
use. Please contact your local bookseller or the Macmillan Corporate and Premium Sales Department at 1-800-221-7945, extension 5442, or by e-mail at
MacmillanSpecialMarkets@macmillan.com.

Third Edition: June 2016

10 9 8 7 6 5 4 3 2 1

Contents

Preface

The authors of this book want you to live a successful and fulfilling life. We also want to enhance your understanding of our fast-changing world. Because your time is valuable, we have crafted this publication in a way that minimizes the time spent learning new terms, memorizing formulas, or mastering intricate details important only to professional economists. Rather, we focus on the general insights of economics that really matter—those that will help you make better choices, improve your understanding of our increasingly complex world, and live a more satisfying life.

Regardless of your current knowledge of economics, this book will provide you with important insights. It is concise, thoughtfully organized, and reader-friendly. It introduces the basic principles of economics, which primarily reflect common sense. The book then puts the principles to work, demonstrating their power to explain real world events and improve our personal decision-making.

The book explains why some nations prosper and others do not. The political process is examined and differences between government and market allocation investigated. Even advanced students of economics and business will find this book valuable because it pulls together the "big picture." You can temporarily set aside the complex formulas, sophisticated models, and technical mathematics of the profession and concentrate on the economic principles that attracted you to economics in the first place.

You will be introduced to a variety of easy-to-use online calculators, spreadsheets, and websites, which will help you take important steps toward financial security. You will be challenged to think about your preferences, choices, and goals. You will also be provided with tools to improve the quality of your life and the value of the services you provide to others.

The authors—the *Common Sense Economics* team—are all economic educators. If you are an economics instructor, we want to help you become a great teacher. To that end, we have developed a multimedia course package to accompany the book. The package takes into account the revealed learning preferences of today's "multimedia" students. It includes short video clips, classic readings, podcasts, innovative assignments, and interactive classroom activities. Visit CommonSenseEconomics.com for details.

The supplementary package accompanying the book is the result of a long-term collaboration with a team of master economic educators dedicated to compiling everything an instructor needs for an exciting introductory course. It incorporates the "read, watch, listen, and do" approach that will help you engage your students and get them excited about economics and personal finance. The book and package meet voluntary K-12 standards and benchmarks. The materials are designed to provide a strong foundation especially for students who may not go on to take another economics course.

Because the *Common Sense Economics* team is anxious to share these materials with economics and personal finance instructors, we offer online courses and special workshops throughout the country. These introduce the full package to teachers and help them learn how to use its content most effectively. If you would like more information on these activities, please consult CommonSenseEconomics.com.

PART 1

*Twelve Key Elements
of Economics*

TWELVE KEY ELEMENTS OF ECONOMICS

1. Incentives matter: Changes in benefits and costs will influence choices in a predictable manner.

2. There is no such thing as a free lunch: Goods are scarce and therefore we have to make choices.

3. Decisions are made at the margin: If we want to get the most out of our resources, options should be chosen only when the marginal benefits exceed the marginal cost.

4. Trade promotes economic progress.

5. Transaction costs are an obstacle to trade.

6. Prices bring the choices of buyers and sellers into balance.

7. Profits direct businesses toward productive activities that increase the value of resources, while losses direct them away from wasteful activities that reduce resource value.

8. People earn income by providing others with things they value.

9. Production of goods and services people value, not just jobs, provides the source of high living standards.

10. Economic progress comes primarily through trade, investment, better ways of doing things, and sound economic institutions.

11. The "invisible hand" of market prices directs buyers and sellers toward activities that promote the general welfare.

12. Too often long-term consequences, or the secondary effects, of an action are ignored.

Introduction

Life is about choices, and economics is about how incentives affect those choices and shape our lives. Choices about our education, how we spend and invest, what we do in the workplace, and many other personal decisions will influence our well-being and quality of life. Moreover, the choices we make as voters and citizens affect the laws or "rules of the game," and these rules exert an enormous impact on our freedom and prosperity. To choose intelligently, both for ourselves and for society generally, we must understand some basic principles about how people choose, what motivates their actions, and how their actions influence their personal welfare and that of others. Thus, economics is about human decision-making, the analysis of the forces underlying choice, and the implications for how societies work.

The economic way of thinking involves the integration of key concepts into your thought process. The following section presents twelve concepts that are crucial for the understanding of economies, and why some countries grow and achieve high income levels while others stagnate and remain poor. You will learn such things as the true meaning of costs, why prices matter, how trade furthers prosperity, and why production of things people value underpins our standard of living. In the subsequent parts of the book, these concepts will be used to address other vitally important topics.

1. Incentives matter: Changes in benefits and costs will influence choices in a predictable manner.

All of economics rests on one simple principle: Changes in incentives influence human behavior in predictable ways. Both monetary and nonmonetary factors influence incentives. If something becomes more costly, people will be less likely to choose it. Correspondingly, when the benefits derived from an option increase, people will be more likely to choose it. This simple idea, sometimes called the basic postulate of economics, is a powerful tool because it applies to almost everything that we do.

People will be less likely to choose an option as it becomes more costly. Think about the implications of this proposition. When late for an appointment, a person will be less likely to take time to stop and visit with a friend. Fewer people will go picnicking on a cold and rainy day. Higher prices will reduce the number of units sold. Attendance in college classes will be below normal the day before spring break. In each case, the explanation is the same: As the option becomes more costly, less is chosen.

Similarly, when the payoff derived from a choice increases, people will be more likely to choose it. A person will be more likely to bend over and pick up a quarter than a penny. Students will attend and pay more attention in class when they know the material will be on the exam. Customers will buy more from stores that offer low prices, high-quality service, and a convenient location. Employees will work harder and more efficiently when they are rewarded for doing so. All of these outcomes are highly predictable and they merely reflect the "incentives matter" postulate of economics.

This basic postulate explains how changes in market prices alter incentives in a manner that works to coordinate the actions of buyers and sellers. If buyers want to purchase more of an item than producers are willing (or able) to sell, its price will soon rise. As the price increases, sellers will be more willing to provide the item while buyers purchase less, until the higher price brings the amount demanded and the amount supplied into balance. At that point the price stabilizes.

What happens if it starts out the other way: if sellers want to supply more than buyers are willing to purchase? If sellers cannot sell all of their goods at the current price, they will have to cut the price of the item. In turn, the lower price will encourage people to buy more—but will also discourage producers from producing as much, since it is less attractive to them to supply the product at the new, lower price. Again, the price change works to bring the amount demanded by consumers into balance with the amount produced by suppliers. At that point there is no further pressure for a price change.

Remember the record-high gas prices in the summer of 2008? While a lot of people felt the pain of higher prices at the pump, there was no panic in the streets or long lines at the gas pumps. Why? When the higher prices made it more costly to purchase gasoline, most consumers eliminated some less important trips. Others arranged more carpooling. With time, consumers also shifted to smaller, more fuel-efficient cars in order to reduce their gasoline bills.

Furthermore, as buyers reacted to higher gas prices, so did sellers. The oil companies supplying gasoline increased their drilling, developed new techniques such as fracking to recover more oil from existing wells, and intensified their search for new oil fields. The higher price helped to keep the quantity supplied in line with the quantity demanded. Eventually, the prices of both crude oil and gasoline fell as supply expanded.

Incentives also influence political choices. There is little reason to believe that a person making choices in the voting booth will behave much differently than when making choices in the shopping mall. In most cases voters are likely to support political candidates and policies that they believe will provide them with the most personal benefits, net of their costs. They will tend to oppose political options when the personal costs are high compared to the benefits they expect to receive. For example, senior citizens have voted numerous times against candidates and proposals that would reduce their Medicare benefits. Similarly, polls indicate that students are strongly supportive of educational grants to college students.

There's no way to get around the importance of incentives. They are a part of human nature. Incentives matter just as much under socialism as under capitalism. In the former Soviet Union, managers and employees of glass plants were at one time rewarded according to the tons of sheet glass they produced. Because their revenues depended on the weight of the glass, most factories produced sheet glass so thick that you could hardly see through it. As a result, the rules were changed so that the managers were compensated according to the number of square meters of glass produced. Under these rules, Soviet firms made glass so thin that it broke easily.

Some people think that incentives matter only when people are greedy and selfish. This is untrue. People act for a variety of reasons, some selfish and some charitable. The choices of both the self-centered and altruistic will be influenced by changes in personal costs and benefits. For example, both the selfish and the altruistic will be more likely to attempt to rescue a child in a shallow swimming pool than in the rapid currents approaching Niagara Falls. And both are more likely to give a needy person their hand-me-downs rather than their best clothes.

Even though no one would have accused the late Mother Teresa of greediness, her self-interest caused her to respond to incentives, too. When Mother Teresa's organization, the Missionaries of Charity, attempted to open a shelter for the homeless in New York City, the city required expensive (but unneeded) alterations to its building. The organization abandoned the project. This decision did not reflect any change in Mother Teresa's commitment to the poor. Instead, it reflected a change in incentives. When the cost of helping the poor in New York went up, Mother Teresa decided that her resources would do more good in other areas.[1] Changes in incentives influence everyone's choices, regardless of the mix of greedy, materialistic goals on the one hand and compassionate, altruistic goals on the other, that drive a specific decision.

2. There is no such thing as a free lunch: Goods are scarce and therefore we have to make choices.

The reality of life on our planet is that productive **resources** are limited, while the human desire for goods and services is virtually unlimited. Would you like to have some new clothes, a luxury boat, or a vacation in the Swiss Alps? How about more time for leisure, recreation, and travel? Do you dream of driving your brand-new Porsche into the driveway of your oceanfront house? Most of us would like to have all of these things and many others! However, we are constrained by the **scarcity** of resources, including a limited availability of time.

Because we cannot have as much of everything as we would like, we are forced to choose among alternatives. There is "no free lunch." Doing one thing makes us sacrifice the opportunity to do something else we value. This is why economists refer to all costs as **opportunity costs**.

Many costs are measured in terms of money, but these too are opportunity costs. The money you spend on one purchase is money that is not available to spend on other things. The opportunity cost of your purchase is the value you place on the items that must now be given up because you spent the money on the initial purchase. But just because

1. Philip K. Howard, *The Death of Common Sense* (New York: Random House, 1994): 3–5.

you don't have to spend money to do something does not mean the action is costless. You don't have to spend money to take a walk and enjoy a beautiful sunset, but there is an opportunity cost to taking the walk. The time you spend walking could have been used to do something else you value, like visiting a friend or reading a book.

It is often said that some things are so important that we should do them without considering the cost. Making such a statement may sound reasonable at first thought, and may be an effective way to encourage people to spend more money on things that we value and for which we would like them to help pay. But the unreasonableness of ignoring cost becomes obvious once we recognize that costs are the value of forgone alternatives (that is, alternatives given up). Saying that we should do something without considering the cost is really saying that we should do it without considering the value of the alternatives. When we choose between mutually exclusive (but equally attractive) alternatives, the least-cost alternative is the best choice.

The choices of both consumers and producers involve costs. As consumers, the cost of a good, as reflected in its price, helps us compare our desire for a product against our desire for alternative products that we could purchase instead. If we do not consider the costs, we will probably end up using our income to purchase the "wrong" things—those goods and services not valued as much as the other items we might have bought.

Producers face costs, too—the costs of the resources used to make a product or provide a service. For example, the use of resources such as lumber, steel, and sheet rock to build a new house takes resources away from the production of other goods, such as hospitals and schools. High costs for resources signal that the resources have other highly valued uses, as judged by buyers and sellers in other markets. Profit-seeking firms will heed those signals and act accordingly, such as seeking out less costly substitutes. However, government policies can override these signals. They can introduce taxes or subsidies that help those inconvenienced by the prices that emerge in free and open markets. But such policies reduce the ability of market incentives to guide resources to where consumers ultimately, on balance, value them most highly.

Politicians, government officials, and lobbyists often speak of "free education," "free medical care," or "free housing." This terminology is deceptive. These things are not free. Scarce resources are required to produce each of them and alternative uses exist. For example, the buildings, labor, and other resources used to produce schooling could instead produce more food, recreation, environmental protection, or medical care. The cost of the schooling is the value of those goods that must be sacrificed. Governments may be able to shift costs, but they cannot eliminate them.

Opportunity cost is an important concept. Everything in life is about opportunity cost. Everyone lives in a world of scarcity and therefore must make choices. By looking at opportunity costs, we can better understand the world in which we live. Consider the impact of opportunity cost on work-force participation, the birth rate, and population growth—topics many would consider outside the realm of opportunity-cost application.

Have you ever thought about why women with more education are more likely to work outside the home than their less-educated counterparts? Opportunity cost provides the answer. The more highly educated women will have better earning opportunities in the workforce, and therefore it will be more costly for them to stay at home. The data are consistent with this view. In 2013, 79.5 percent of women aged twenty-five to sixty-four with a college education (or more) were in the labor force, compared to only 64.4 percent of their counterparts with only a high school education and 46 percent of the women with less than twelve years of schooling.[2] Just as economic theory predicts, when it is more

2. "Women in the Labor Force: A Databook." *BLS Reports* 1052 (2014): 27. U.S. Bureau of Labor Statistics (December 2014). www.bls.gov/opub/reports/cps/women-in-the-labor-force-a-databook-2014.pdf.

costly for a woman to be out of the labor force, fewer will choose this option.

What do you think happens to the birth rate as an economy grows and earnings rise? Time spent on household responsibilities reduces the time available for market work. As earnings rise, the opportunity cost of having children and raising a large family increases. Therefore, the predicted result is a reduction in the birth rate and slower population growth. The real world reflects this analysis. During the past two centuries, as the per capita income of a country increased, a reduction in the birth rate and a slowdown in population growth soon followed. Moreover, this pattern has occurred in every country. Even though there are widespread cultural, religious, ethnic, and political organizational differences among countries, nonetheless the higher opportunity cost of having children exerted the same impact on the birth rate in all cases.

Opportunity cost is a powerful tool and it will be applied again and again throughout this book. If you integrate this tool into your thought process, it will greatly enhance your ability to understand the real-world behavior of consumers, producers, business owners, political figures, and other decision-makers. Even more important, the concept will also help you make better choices.

3. *Decisions are made at the margin: If we want to get the most out of our resources, options should be chosen only when the marginal benefits exceed the marginal cost.*

If we are going to get the most out of our resources, actions should be undertaken when they generate more benefits than costs and rejected when they are more costly than the benefits derived. This principle of sound decision-making applies to individuals, businesses, government officials, and society as a whole.

Nearly all choices are made at the margin. That means that they almost always involve additions to (or subtractions from) current conditions, rather than "all-or-nothing" decisions. The word "additional" is a substitute for "**marginal**." We might ask, "What is the marginal (or additional) cost of producing or purchasing one more unit?" Marginal decisions may involve large or small changes. The "one more unit" could be a new shirt, a new house, a new factory, or even an expenditure of time, as in the case of a high school or college student choosing among various activities. All these decisions are marginal because they involve consideration of additional costs and benefits.

People do not make "all-or-nothing" decisions, such as choosing between eating or wearing clothes. Instead they compare the marginal benefits (a little more food) with the marginal costs (a little less clothing or a little less of something else). In making decisions individuals don't compare the total value of food and the total value of clothing, but rather they compare their marginal values. Further, we choose options only when the marginal benefits exceed the marginal costs.

Similarly, a business executive planning to build a new factory will consider whether the **marginal benefits** of the new factory (for example, additional sales revenues) are greater than the **marginal costs** (the expense of constructing the new building). If not, the executive and the company are better off without the new factory.

Effective political actions also require marginal decision-making. Consider the political decision of how much effort should go into cleaning up pollution. If asked how much pollution we should allow, many people would respond "none"—in other words, we should reduce pollution to zero. In the voting booth they might vote that way. But marginal thinking reveals that this would be extraordinarily wasteful.

When there is a lot of pollution— so much, say, that we are choking on the air we breathe—the marginal benefit of reducing pollution is quite likely to exceed the marginal cost of the reduction. But as the amount of pollution goes down, so does the marginal benefit—the value of the additional improvement in the air. There is still a benefit to an even cleaner atmosphere (for example, we would be able to see distant mountains) but this benefit is not nearly as valuable as protecting our lungs. At some point before all pollution disappeared, the marginal benefit of eliminating more pollution would decline to almost zero.

As pollution is being reduced, the marginal benefit is going down while the marginal cost is going up and becomes very high before all pollution is eliminated. The marginal cost is the value of other things that have to be sacrificed to reduce pollution a little bit more. Once the marginal cost of a cleaner atmosphere exceeds the marginal benefit, additional pollution reduction would be wasteful. It would simply not be worth the cost.

To continue with the pollution example, consider the following hypothetical situation. Assume that we know that pollution is doing $100 million worth of damage, and only $1 million is being spent to reduce pollution. Given this information, are we doing too little, or too much, to reduce pollution? Most people would say that we are spending too little. This may be correct, but it doesn't follow from the information given.

The $100 million in damage is total damage, and the $1 million in cost is the total cost of cleanup. To make an informed decision about what to do next, we need to know the marginal benefit of cleanup and the marginal cost of doing so. If spending another $10 on pollution reduction would reduce damage by more than $10, then we should spend more. The marginal benefit exceeds the marginal cost. But if an additional $10 spent on antipollution efforts would reduce damages by only a dollar, additional antipollution spending would be unwise.

People commonly ignore the implications of marginalism in their comments and votes but seldom in their personal actions. Consider food versus recreation. When viewed as a whole, food is far more valuable than recreation because it allows people to survive. When people are poor and living in impoverished countries, they devote most of their income to securing an adequate diet. They devote little time, if any, to playing golf, water skiing, or other recreational activities.

But as people become wealthier, the opportunity cost of acquiring food declines. Although food remains vital to life, continuing to spend most of their money on food would be foolish. At higher levels of affluence, people find that at the margin—as they make decisions about how to spend each additional dollar—food is worth much less than recreation. So as Americans become wealthier, they spend a smaller portion of their income on food and a larger portion of their income on recreation.[3]

The concept of marginalism reveals that it is the marginal costs and marginal benefits that are relevant to sound decision-making. If we want to get the most out of our resources, we must undertake only actions that provide marginal benefits that are equal to or greater than marginal costs. Both individuals and nations will be more prosperous when their choices reflect the implications of marginalism.

4. Trade promotes economic progress.

The foundation of trade is mutual gain. People agree to an exchange because they expect it to improve their well-being. The motivation for trade is summed up in the statement: "If you do something good for me, I will do something good for you." Trade is a win-win transaction. This positive-sum activity permits each of the trading partners to get more of what they value. There are three major sources of gains from trade.

First, trade moves goods from people who value them less to people who value them more. Thus, trade can increase the value of goods even when nothing new is produced. For example, when used goods are sold

3. See the chapter "Time for Symphonies and Softball" in W. Michael Cox and Richard Alm, *Myths of Rich and Poor* (New York: Basic Books, 1999).

at flea markets, through Craigslist, or over the Internet, the exchanges do not increase the quantity of goods available (as new products do). But the trades move products toward people who value them more. Both the buyer and seller gain, or otherwise the exchange would not occur.

People's preferences, knowledge, and goals vary widely. A product that is virtually worthless to one person may be a precious gem to another. A highly technical book on electronics may be worth nothing to an art collector but valued at hundreds of dollars by an engineer. Similarly, a painting that an engineer cares little for may be cherished by an art collector. Voluntary exchange that moves the electronics book to the engineer and the painting to the art collector will increase the benefit derived from both goods. The trade will increase the wealth of both people and also their nation. It is not just the amount of goods and services produced in a nation that determines the nation's wealth, but how those goods and services are allocated.

Second, trade makes larger production and consumption levels possible because it allows each of us to specialize more fully in the things that we do best relative to cost. When people specialize, they can then sell these products to others. Revenues received can be used to purchase items that would be costly to produce themselves. Through these exchanges, people who specialize in this way will produce a larger total quantity of goods and services than would otherwise be possible. Economists refer to this principle as the **law of comparative advantage.** This law applies to trade among individuals, businesses, regions, and nations.

The law of comparative advantage is just common sense. If someone else is willing to provide you with a product at a lower cost (keep in mind that all costs are opportunity costs) than you can provide it for yourself, it makes sense to trade for it. You can then use your time and resources to produce more of the things for which you are a low-cost producer. In other words, produce what you produce best, and trade for the rest. The result is that you and your trading partners will mutually gain from specialization and trade, leading to greater total production and higher incomes. In contrast, trying to produce everything yourself would mean you are using your time and resources to produce many things for which you are a high-cost provider. This would translate into lower production and income.

For example, even though most doctors might be good at record keeping and arranging appointments, it is generally in their interest to hire someone to perform these services. The time doctors use to keep records is time they could have spent seeing patients. Because the time spent with their patients is worth a lot, the opportunity cost of record keeping for doctors will be high. Thus, doctors will almost always find it advantageous to hire someone else to keep and manage their records. Moreover, when the doctor specializes in the provision of physician services and hires someone who has a comparative advantage in record keeping, costs will be lower and joint output larger than would otherwise be achieveable.

Third, voluntary exchange allows firms to achieve lower per-unit costs by adopting large-scale production methods. Trade makes it possible for business firms to sell their output over a broad market area so they can plan for large outputs and adopt manufacturing processes that take advantage of **economies of scale**. Such processes often lead to substantially lower per-unit costs and enormous increases in output per worker. Without trade, these gains could not be achieved. Market forces are continuously reallocating production toward low-cost producers (and away from high-cost ones). As a result, open markets tend to allocate products and resources in ways that maximize the value, amount, and variety of the goods and services that are produced.

The importance of trade in our modern world can hardly be exaggerated. Trade makes it possible for most of us to consume a bundle of goods and services far beyond what we would be able to produce for ourselves. Can you imagine the difficulty involved in producing your own housing, clothing, and food, to say nothing of computers, television sets, dishwashers, automobiles, and telephones? People who have these things have them largely because their economies are organized in such a way that individuals can cooperate, specialize, and trade. Countries that impose obstacles to exchange—either domestic or international—reduce the ability of their citizens to achieve gains from trade and to live more prosperous lives.

5. *Transaction costs are an obstacle to trade.*

Voluntary exchange promotes cooperation and helps us get more of what we want. However, trade itself is costly. It takes time, effort, and other resources to search out potential trading partners, negotiate trades, and close the sale. Resources spent in this way are called **transaction costs,** and they are an obstacle to the creation of wealth. They limit both our productive capacity and the realization of gains from mutually advantageous trades.

Transaction costs are sometimes high because of physical obstacles, such as oceans, rivers, and mountains, which make it difficult to get products to customers. Investment in roads and improvements in transportation and communications can reduce these transaction costs. In other instances, transaction costs may be high because of the lack of information. For example, you may want to buy a used copy of the economics book assigned for a class, but you don't know who has a copy and is willing to sell it at an attractive price. You need to track down someone willing to sell a used copy: the time and energy you spend doing so is part of your transaction costs. In still other cases, transaction costs are high because of political obstacles, such as taxes, licensing requirements, government regulations, price controls, tariffs, or quotas. Regardless of whether the roadblocks are physical, informational, or political, high transaction costs reduce the potential gains from trade.

People who help others arrange trades and make better choices reduce transaction costs and promote economic progress. Such specialists, sometimes called middlemen, include campus bookstores, real estate agents, stockbrokers, automobile dealers, and a wide variety of merchants. Many believe that middlemen merely increase the price of goods and services without providing benefits. If this were true, people would not use their services. Transaction costs are an obstacle to trade, and middlemen reduce these costs. This is why people value their services.

The grocer, for example, is a middleman. (Of course, today's giant supermarket reflects the actions of many people, but together their services are those of a middleman.) Think of the time and effort that would be involved in preparing even a single meal if shoppers had to deal directly with farmers when purchasing vegetables, citrus growers when buying fruit, dairy operators if they wanted milk or cheese, and ranchers or fishermen if they wanted to serve beef or fish. Grocers make these contacts for consumers, place the items in a convenient selling location, and maintain reliable inventories. The services of grocers and other middlemen reduce transaction costs significantly, making it easier for potential buyers and sellers to realize gains from trade. These services increase the volume of trade and promote economic progress.

In recent years, technology has reduced the transaction costs of numerous exchanges. With just a few swipes on a touch screen, buyers can now acquire information about potential sellers of almost every product. Apps are routinely used to shop for movies, clothing, and household goods, locate a hotel room, obtain tickets for a major concert or big football game, and even hail a taxi. These reductions in transaction costs have increased the volume of trade and enhanced our living standards.

6. Prices bring the choices of buyers and sellers into balance.

Market prices will influence the choices of both buyers and sellers. When a rise in the price of a good makes it more expensive for buyers to purchase it, they will normally choose to buy fewer units. Thus, there is a negative relationship between the price of a good or service and the quantity demanded. This negative relationship is known as the **law of demand**.

For sellers, the rise in the price of that product brings extra revenue that makes them willing to supply more of it. Thus, there is a positive relationship between the price of a good and the quantity producers will supply. This positive relationship is known as the **law of supply**.

Economists often use graphics to illustrate the relationships among price, quantity demanded, and quantity supplied. When doing so, the price of a good is placed on the vertical y-axis and the quantity per unit of time (for example, a week, month, or year) on the horizontal x-axis. Using ice cream as an example, Exhibit 1 illustrates the classic demand and supply graphic. The demand curve indicates the various quantities of ice cream consumers will purchase at alternative prices. Note how the demand curve slopes downward to the right, indicating that consumers will purchase more ice cream as its price declines. This is merely a graphic representation of the law of demand.

The supply curve indicates the various quantities of ice cream producers are willing to supply at alternative prices. As Exhibit 1 illustrates, it slopes upward to the right, indicating that producers will be willing to supply larger quantities at higher prices. The supply curve provides a graphic representation of the law of supply.

Now for a really important point: The price will tend to move toward a level, $3 per quart of ice cream in our example, that will bring the quantity demanded into equality with the quantity supplied. At the **equilibrium** price of $3, consumers will want to purchase 15 thousand

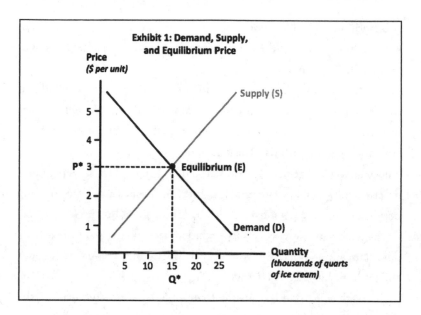

Exhibit 1: Demand, Supply, and Equilibrium Price

quarts of ice cream per day, the same quantity that ice cream producers are willing to supply. Price coordinates the choices of both consumers and producers of ice cream and brings them into balance.

If the price is higher than $3, for example $4, producers will want to supply more ice cream than consumers will want to purchase. At the $4 price, producers will be unable to sell as many units as they would like. Inventories will rise and this excess supply will lead some producers to cut their price to reduce their excess inventories. The price will tend to decline until the $3 equilibrium price is reached. It is easy to see, then, that if the price is above the equilibrium, market forces will push price down toward equilibrium.

Correspondingly, if the price of ice cream is less than $3, for example $2, consumers will want to purchase a larger quantity than producers are willing to supply. This generates excess demand and will place upward pressure on price and it will tend to move back toward the equilibrium of $3. The choices of buyers and sellers will be consistent with each other only at the equilibrium price and the market price will gravitate toward this level.

The auction system on eBay illustrates the operation of demand and supply in a setting that is familiar to many. On eBay, sellers enter their reserve prices—the minimum prices they will accept for goods; buyers enter their maximum bids—the maximum prices they are willing to pay. The auction management system will bid on behalf of the buyers in pre-determined monetary increments. Bidding ensues until the trading period expires or a person agrees to pay the stated "Buy it Now" price. Exchange occurs only when buyers bid a price greater than the seller's minimum asking price. But when this happens, an exchange will occur and both the buyer and seller will gain.

Though somewhat less visible than the eBay electronic market, the forces of demand and supply in other markets work similarly. The height of the demand curve indicates the maximum amount the consumer is willing to pay for another unit of the good, while the height of the supply curve shows the minimum price at which producers are willing to supply another unit. As long as the price is between the maximum the consumer is willing to pay and the minimum offer price of a seller, potential gains from trade are present. Moreover, when the equilibrium price is present, all potential gains from exchange will be realized.

Thus, consumers will tend to purchase only units that they value more than the actual price. Similarly, producers will supply only units that can be produced at a cost less than that price. When the equilibrium price is present, units will be produced and purchased as long as the value of the good to consumers exceeds the cost of the resources required for its production. The implication: Market prices not only bring the quantity demanded and quantity supplied into balance, but they also direct producers to supply those goods that consumers value more than their cost of production. This holds true in any market.

Of course, we live in a dynamic world. Through time, changes will occur that will alter the demand and supply of goods and services. Factors such as consumer income, prices of related goods, the expectation of a future price increase, and the number of consumers in the market area will influence the market demand for a good. Changes in any of these factors will alter the amount of a good consumers will want to purchase at alternative prices. Put another way, changes in these factors will cause a change in demand, a shift in the entire demand curve. It is important to distinguish between a change in demand—a shift in the entire demand curve, and a change in quantity demanded—a movement along a demand curve as the result of a change in the price of the good. (Important note to students: Failure to distinguish between a change in demand and a change in quantity demanded is one of the most common errors in all of economics. Moreover, questions on this topic are favorites of many economics instructors. Wise students will take this note seriously.)

Exhibit 2 illustrates the impact of an increase in demand on the market price of a good. Suppose there is an increase in consumers' income or a rise in the price of frozen yogurt, a common substitute for ice cream. These changes will increase the demand for ice cream, causing the demand curve to shift to the right from D_1 to D_2. In turn, the stronger demand will push the equilibrium price of ice cream upward from \$3 to \$4. At the new higher equilibrium price, the quantity demanded by consumers will once again be brought into balance with the quantity supplied by producers. Note, the increase in demand (shift in the entire demand curve) will result in an increase in the quantity supplied from 15 thousand to 20 thousand, a movement along the existing supply curve.

A reduction in consumer income or lower frozen yogurt prices would exert the opposite impact. These changes would reduce the demand for ice cream (shift the demand curve to the left), lower the price, and reduce the equilibrium quantity exchanged.

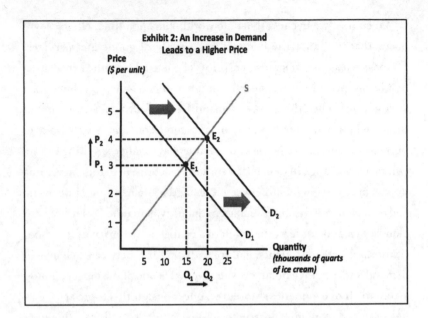

Exhibit 2: An Increase in Demand Leads to a Higher Price

Now let's turn to the supply side of a market. Changes in factors that alter the per-unit cost of supplying a good will cause the entire supply curve to shift. Changes that lower per-unit costs (for example, an improvement in technology, lower prices for the resources used to produce the good or subsidies to the producers) will increase supply, causing the entire supply curve to shift to the right. In contrast, changes that make it more expensive to produce the good, such as higher prices for the required ingredients or higher taxes imposed on the producers will reduce supply, causing the supply curve to shift to the left.

Suppose there is a reduction in the prices of cream and milk, ingredients used to produce ice cream. What impact will these resource price reductions have on the supply and market price of ice cream? If your answer is supply will increase and the market price decline, you are correct. Exhibit 3 illustrates this point within the demand and supply framework. The lower prices of cream and milk will reduce the per-unit cost of producing ice cream, causing the supply curve to shift to the right (from S_1 to S_2). As a result, the equilibrium price of ice cream will decline from $3 to $2. At the new lower price, the quantity demanded will increase and once again equal the quantity supplied at 20 thousand quarts per day. Note: The increase in supply (the shift of the entire curve) lowered the price of ice cream and increased the quantity demanded—a movement along the existing demand curve. If changes occurred that increased the cost of producing ice cream (for example, higher prices for the ingredients), the results would be just the opposite: a decrease in supply (shift to the left), increase in the price of ice cream, and a reduction in the quantity exchanged.

Market adjustments like the ones outlined here will not take place instantaneously. It will take time for both consumers and producers to adjust fully to the new conditions. In fact, in a dynamic world, the adjustment process is continuous. The impact of changes in demand and supply and factors that underlie shifts in these curves are central to the understanding of the market process. Demand and supply analysis will

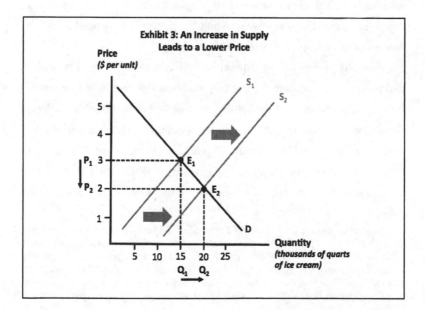

Exhibit 3: An Increase in Supply Leads to a Lower Price

be utilized again and again throughout this book. The website accompanying this text—CommonSenseEconomics.com—contains a free supplementary reading, "Demand, Supply, and Adjustments to Dynamic Change." It provides additional analysis of shifts in demand and supply and the impact of various types of dynamic changes on the market price.

7. *Profits direct businesses toward productive activities that increase the value of resources, while losses direct them away from wasteful activities that reduce resource value.*

Businesses purchase natural resources, labor, capital, and entrepreneurial talent. These **productive resources** are then transformed into goods and services that are sold to consumers. In a market economy, producers will have to bid resources away from their alternative uses because the owners of the resources will supply them only at prices at least equal to what they could earn elsewhere. The producer's opportunity cost of supplying a good or service will equal the payments required to bid the resources away from their other potential uses.

There is an important difference between the opportunity cost of production and standard accounting measures of cost. Accountants focus on the calculation of the firm's net income, which is slightly different than economic **profit**. The net income calculation omits the opportunity cost of assets owned by the firm. While accountants omit this opportunity cost, economists do not.[4] As a result, the firm's net income will overstate profit, as measured by the economist. Economists consider the

4. For example, if a corporation invests $100 million in buildings and equipment to produce a product, it is forgoing the earnings these funds could have earned if invested in other ways. The corporation could have simply put the $100 million in the bank and let it draw interest at say, a 5 percent rate. In a year's time, the interest earnings would sum to $5 million. This $5 million in forgone interest is an opportunity cost of the activities of the corporation, but it will not be reflected on the firm's accounting statement. Because

fact that the assets owned by the firm could be used some other way. Unless these opportunity costs are covered, the resources will eventually be used in other ways.

A firm's profit can be determined in the following manner:

Profit = Total Revenue − Total Cost

The firm's total revenue is simply the sales price of all goods sold (P) times the quantity (Q) of all goods sold. In order to earn a profit, a firm must generate more revenue from the sale of its product than the opportunity cost of the resources required to make the good. Thus, a firm will earn a profit only if it is able to produce a good or service that consumers value more than the cost of the resources required for their production.

Consumers will not purchase a good unless they value it as much, or more, than the price. If consumers are willing to pay more than the production costs, then the decision by the producer to bid the resources away from their alternative uses will have been a profitable one. Profit is a reward for transforming resources into something of greater value.

Business decision-makers will seek to undertake production of goods and services that will generate profit. However, things do not always turn out as expected. Sometimes business firms are unable to sell their products at prices that will cover their costs. **Losses** occur when the total revenue from sales is less than the opportunity cost of the resources used to produce a good or service. Losses are a penalty imposed on businesses that produce goods and services that consumers value less than the resources required for their production. The losses indicate that the resources would have been better used producing other things.

Suppose it costs a shirt manufacturer $20,000 per month to lease a

---

of this omission, accounting costs understate the opportunity costs of the resources utilized. Therefore, net income overstates profit.

building, rent the required machines, and purchase the labor, cloth, buttons, and other materials necessary to produce and market one thousand shirts per month. If the manufacturer sells the one thousand shirts for $22 each, he receives $22,000 in monthly revenue, or $2,000 in profit. The shirt manufacturer has created wealth—for himself and for the consumer. By their willingness to pay more than the costs of production, his customers reveal that they value the shirts more than they value the resources required for their production. The manufacturer's profit is a reward for increasing the value of resources by converting them into the more highly valued product.

On the other hand, if the demand for shirts declines and they can be sold only for $17 each, then the manufacturer will earn $17,000, losing $3,000 a month. This loss occurs because the manufacturer's actions reduced the value of the resources used. The shirts—the final product—were worth less to consumers than the value of other things that could have been produced with the resources. We are not saying that consumers consciously know that the resources used to make the shirts would have been more valuable if converted into some other product. But their combined choices provide this information to the manufacturer, along with the incentive to take steps to reduce the loss.

In a market economy, losses and business failures work constantly to bring inefficient activities—such as producing shirts that sell for less than their cost—to a halt. Losses and business failures will redirect the resources toward the production of other goods that are valued more highly. Thus, even though business failures are often painful for the owners, investors, and employees involved, there is a positive side: They release resources that can be directed toward wealth-creating projects.

The people of a nation will be better off if their resources—their land, buildings, labor, and entrepreneurial talent—produce valuable goods and services. At any given time a virtually unlimited number of potential investment projects are available to be undertaken. Some of these investments will increase the value of resources by transforming them into goods and services that consumers value highly relative to cost. These will promote economic progress. Other investments will reduce the value of resources and reduce economic progress. If we are going to get the most out of the available resources, projects that increase value must be encouraged, while those that use resources less productively must be discouraged. This is precisely what profits and losses do.

We live in a world of changing tastes and technology, imperfect knowledge, and uncertainty. Business owners cannot be sure what the future market prices will be or what the future costs of production will be. Their decisions are based on expectations. But the reward-penalty structure of a market economy is clear. **Entrepreneurs** who produce efficiently and who anticipate correctly the goods and services that attract consumers at prices above production cost will prosper. In contrast, business executives who allocate resources inefficiently into areas where demand is weak will be penalized with losses and financial difficulties.

While some criticize the business failures that accompany the market process, this reward-penalty system underlies the prosperity that markets provide. Interestingly, many of the entrepreneurs who initially failed eventually succeed in a big way. Steve Jobs provides an example. After leaving Apple in 1985, Jobs founded neXT, a firm that he thought would produce the next generation of personal computers. The company struggled. But, Jobs learned from the experience. He returned to Apple in 1997 and soon introduced the iPhone, the iPad, and other innovative products that succeeded spectacularly in the marketplace.

The bottom line is straightforward: Profits direct business investment toward productive projects that promote economic progress, while losses channel resources away from projects that are counterproductive.

This is a vitally important function. Economies that fail to perform this function well will almost surely experience stagnation, or worse.

8. *People earn income by providing others with things they value.*

People differ in many ways—in their productive abilities, preferences, specialized skills, attitudes, and willingness to take risks. These differences influence people's incomes because they affect the value of the goods and services that individuals are willing and able to provide to others.

In a market economy, people who earn high incomes do so because they provide others with things they value more than their cost. If these individuals did not provide valuable goods or services, consumers would not pay them so generously. There is a moral here: If you want to earn a high income, you had better figure out how to help others a great deal. On the other hand, if you are unable or unwilling to help others in ways they value, your income will be low.

This direct link between helping others and receiving income gives each of us a strong incentive to acquire skills, develop talents, and cultivate habits that will help us provide others with valuable goods and services. College students study for long hours, endure stress, and incur the financial cost of schooling in order to become doctors, teachers, accountants, and engineers. Other people acquire training, certification, and experience that will help them become electricians, maintenance workers, or website designers. Still others invest and start businesses. Why do people do these things?

In some cases individuals may be motivated by a strong personal desire to improve the world. However—and this is the key point—even people who don't care about improving the world, who are motivated mostly by the desire for income, will have a strong incentive to develop skills and take actions that are valuable to others. High earnings come from providing goods and services that others value. People seeking great wealth will have a strong incentive to pay close attention to what others want. And even those people who want to improve the world need information on the education and skills they can acquire, which will do the most to make the world a better place for others. This information is generally provided by the earning opportunities in different occupations.

Some people think that high-income individuals must be exploiting others. But people who earn high incomes in the marketplace generally do so by providing others with things they value and for which they are willing to pay. Mark Zuckerberg, one of the founders of Facebook, earned billions of dollars because the social networking website Facebook provided an enhanced communication tool to hundreds of millions of people worldwide. As of the first quarter of 2015, there were approximately 1.4 billion Facebook subscribers. Popular singers provide another example. Beyoncé and Taylor Swift each have huge earnings because millions enjoy their music.

Business entrepreneurs who succeed in a big way do so by making products that millions of consumers find attractive. The late Sam Walton, who founded Walmart, became one of the richest men in the United States because he figured out how to manage large inventories effectively and sell brand-name merchandise at discount prices to small-town America. Bill Gates and Paul Allen, cofounders of Microsoft, became billionaires by developing a set of products that dramatically improved the efficiency and compatibility of desktop computers. Millions of consumers who never heard of Zuckerberg, Walton, Gates, or Allen benefited from their talents and products. They made a lot of money because they helped a lot of people.

9. Production of goods and services people value, not just jobs, provides the source of high living standards.

Consumption is the sole end and purpose of all production; and the interest of the producer ought to be attended to only so far as it may be necessary for promoting that of the consumer.[5]

—ADAM SMITH (1776)

As Adam Smith noted some 240 years ago, consumption is the objective of all production. But, consumption comes before production only in the dictionary. Income and living standards cannot increase without an increase in the production of goods and services that people value.

Clearly, destroying commonly traded goods that people value will make a society worse off. This proposition is so intuitively obvious that it almost seems silly to highlight it. But policies based on the fallacious idea that destroying goods will benefit society have sometimes been adopted. In 1933, Congress passed the Agricultural Adjustment Act (AAA) in an effort to reduce supply and thus prevent the prices of agricultural products from falling. Under this New Deal legislation, the federal government paid farmers to plow under portions of their cotton, corn, wheat, and other crops. Potato farmers were paid to spray their potatoes with dye so they would be unfit for human consumption. Healthy cattle, sheep, and pigs were slaughtered and buried in mass graves in order to keep them off of the market. Six million baby pigs were killed under the AAA in 1933 alone. The Supreme Court declared the act unconstitutional in 1936, but not before it had kept millions of valuable agricultural products from American consumers. Moreover,

5. Adam Smith, *An Inquiry into the Nature and Causes of the Wealth of Nations,* Volume II Glasgow Edition (Indianapolis: Liberty Fund, Inc., [1776] 1981): 660. Also available at: www.econlib.org/library/Smith/smWN.html.

under modified forms of the Act, even today the government continues to pay various farmers to limit their production. While the political demands of those benefiting from the policies are understandable, such programs destroy valuable resources, making the nation poorer.

The 2009 "Cash for Clunkers" program provides another example of politicians attempting to promote prosperity by destroying productive assets—used cars in this case. Under the Cash for Clunkers program, car dealers were paid between $3,500 and $4,500 to destroy the older cars that were traded in for a new automobile. Dealers were required to ruin the car engines with a sodium silicate solution, then smash them and send them to the junkyard, assuring that not even the parts would be available for future use. The proponents of this program argued that it would stimulate recovery by inducing people to buy new cars. But the new cars cost more than used ones, and the price of used ones increased because of the decline in supply. As a result, consumers spent more on automobiles (both new and used) and therefore less was available for spending on other items. Thus, the Cash for Clunkers program failed to stimulate total demand. In essence, taxpayers provided $3 billion in subsidies for new car purchases, while destroying approximately 700,000 used cars valued at about $2 billion. Those who could afford new cars were subsidized, while poor people who depend on used cars were punished. And new car sales plunged when the program expired.

If destroying automobiles is a good idea, why not require owners to destroy their automobile every year? Think of all of the new-car sales this would generate. All of this is unsound economics. You may be able to help specific producers by increasing the scarcity of their products, but you cannot make the general populace better off by destroying marketable goods with consumption value.

A more subtle form of destruction involves government actions that increase the opportunity cost of obtaining various goods. For example, the federal government has subsidized the production of ethanol even though it costs about $1.50 more per gallon than the energy equivalent of gasoline. These subsidies increase our cost of obtaining energy and most experts also believe that they push up food prices and exert an adverse impact on the environment. But they provide highly visible benefits to corn farmers in the important presidential primary state of Iowa, and this will make them difficult to repeal.

Politicians and proponents of government spending projects are fond of boasting about the jobs created by their spending programs and they exaggerate program benefits. This makes economic literacy particularly important. While employment is often used as a means to create wealth, we must remember that it is not simply more jobs that improve our economic well-being but rather jobs that produce goods and services people value. When that elementary fact is forgotten, people are often misled into acceptance of programs that reduce wealth rather than create it.

The focus on creating jobs can be extremely misleading, as an apocryphal story about an engineer visiting China illustrates. He came across a large crew of men building a dam with picks and shovels. When the engineer pointed out to the supervisor that the job could be completed in a few days, rather than many months, if the men were given motorized earthmoving equipment, the supervisor said that such equipment would destroy many jobs. "Oh," the engineer responded, "I thought you were interested in building a dam. If it's more jobs you want, why don't you have your men use spoons instead of shovels?"

10. Economic progress comes primarily through trade, investment, better ways of doing things, and sound economic institutions.

On the first day of an introductory economics class, we often inform students that Americans produce and earn approximately thirty times as much per person today as in 1750. Then we solicit their views on the following question: "Why are Americans so much more productive today than two and a half centuries ago?" Think for a moment how you would respond to this question.

Invariably, our students mention three things: First, today's scientific knowledge and technological abilities are far beyond anything Americans imagined in 1750. Second, we have complex machines and factories, far better roads, and extensive systems of communications. Finally, students usually mention that in 1750 individuals and families directly produced most of the items that they consumed, whereas today we typically purchase them from others.

Basically, the students provide the correct explanation even though they have little or no prior knowledge of economics. They recognize the importance of technology, capital (productive assets), and trade. Their response reinforces our view that economics is the "science of common sense."

We have already highlighted gains from trade and the importance of reducing transaction costs as sources of economic progress. Economic analysis pinpoints three other sources of economic growth: investments in people and productive assets, improvements in technology, and improvements in economic organization.

First, investments in **physical capital** (such as tools, machines, and buildings) and **human capital** (education, skills, training, and experience of workers) enhance our ability to produce goods and services. The two kinds of investment are linked. Workers can produce more if they work with more and better machines. A logger can produce more when working with a chainsaw rather than a hand-operated, crosscut blade. Similarly, a transport worker can haul more with a truck than with a mule and wagon.

Second, improvements in technology (the use of brain power to discover new products and less costly methods of production) spur economic progress. Since 1750, the steam engine, followed by the internal combustion engine, electricity, and nuclear power replaced human and animal power as the major source of energy. Automobiles, buses, trains, and airplanes replaced the horse and buggy (and walking) as the chief methods of transportation. Technological improvements continue to change our lifestyles. Consider the impact of personal computers, microwave ovens, cell phones, streaming programs on TV, heart by-pass surgery, hip replacements, automobile air conditioners, and even garage door openers. The introduction and development of these products during the last fifty years have vastly changed the way that we work, play, and entertain ourselves. They have improved our well-being.

Third, improvements in economic organization can promote growth. By economic organization we mean the ways that human activities are organized and the rules under which they operate—factors often taken for granted or overlooked. How easy is it for people to engage in trade or to organize a business? The legal system of a country, to a large extent, determines the level of trade, investment, and economic cooperation undertaken by the residents of a nation. A legal system that protects individuals and their property, enforces contracts fairly, and settles disputes is an essential ingredient for economic progress. Without it, investment will be lacking, trade will be stifled, and the spread of innovative ideas will be impeded. Part 2 of this book will examine in more detail the importance of the legal structure and other elements of economic organization.

Investment and improvements in technology do not just happen. They reflect the actions of entrepreneurs, people who take risks in the hope of profit. No one knows what the next innovative breakthrough will be or just which production techniques will reduce costs. Furthermore, entrepreneurs are often found in unexpected places. Thus, economic progress depends on a system that allows a very diverse set of people to test their ideas to see if they are profitable and, simultaneously, discourages them from squandering resources on unproductive projects.

For this progress to occur, markets must be open so that individuals are free to try their innovative ideas. An entrepreneur with a new product or technology needs to win the support of only enough investors to finance the project. But, **competition** must be present to hold entrepreneurs and their investors accountable for the efficient allocation of their resources: Their ideas must face the "reality check" of consumers who will decide whether or not to purchase a product or service at a price above the production cost. In this environment, consumers are the ultimate judge and jury. If they do not value an innovative product or service enough to cover its cost, it will not survive in the marketplace.

11. The "invisible hand" of market prices directs buyers and sellers toward activities that promote the general welfare.

Every individual is continually exerting himself to find out the most advantageous employment for whatever capital he can command. It is his own advantage, indeed, and not that of the society which he has in view. But the study of his own advantage naturally, or rather necessarily, leads him to prefer that employment which is most advantageous to society. He intends only his own gain, and he is in this, as in many other cases, led by an invisible hand to promote an end which was not part of his intention.[6]

—ADAM SMITH (1776)

Self-interest is a powerful motivator. As Adam Smith noted long ago, when directed by the **invisible hand,** self-interested individuals will have a strong incentive to undertake actions that promote the general

6. Adam Smith, ibid.: 454.

prosperity of a community or nation. The "invisible hand" to which Smith refers is the price system. The individual "intends only his own gain" but he is directed by the invisible hand of market prices to promote the goals of others, leading to greater prosperity.

The principle of the "invisible hand" is difficult for many people to grasp. There is a natural tendency to perceive that orderly outcomes can only be achieved when someone is in charge or through directions from a centralized authority. Yet Adam Smith contended that pursuing one's own advantage creates an orderly society in which demands are routinely satisfied without centralized planning. This order occurs because market prices coordinate the actions of self-interested individuals when private property and freedom of exchange are present. One statistic—the current market price of a particular good or service—provides buyers and sellers with what they need to bring their actions into harmony with the best possible information on the current actions and preferences of others. Market prices register the choices of millions of consumers, producers, and resource suppliers. They reflect information about consumer preferences, costs, and matters related to timing, location, and circumstances—information that in any large market is well beyond the comprehension of any individual or central-planning authority.

Have you ever wondered why the supermarkets in your community have approximately the right amount of milk, bread, vegetables, and other goods—an amount large enough that the goods are nearly always available but not so large that a lot gets spoiled or wasted? How is it that refrigerators, automobiles, and touch screen tablets, produced at diverse places around the world, are available in your local market in about the quantity that consumers desire? Where is the technical manual for businesses to follow to get this done? Of course, there is no manual. The invisible hand of market prices provides the answer. It directs self-interested individuals into cooperative action and brings their choices into line with each other through price signaling as described in Element 6.

The 1974 Nobel Prize recipient Friedrich Hayek called the market system a "marvel" because just one indicator, the market price of a commodity, spontaneously carries so much information that it guides buyers and sellers to make decisions that help both obtain what they want.[7] The market price of a product reflects thousands, even millions, of decisions made around the world by people who don't know what the others are doing. For each product or service, the market acts like a giant computer network grinding out an indicator that gives all participants both the information they need and the incentive to act on it.

No individual or central-planning authority could possibly obtain or consider all the information needed for millions of consumers and producers of thousands of different goods and services to coordinate their actions the way markets do. Moreover, market prices contain this information in a distilled form. They will direct producers and resource suppliers toward production of those things that consumers value most (relative to their costs). No one will have to force a farmer to raise apples or tell a construction firm to build houses or convince a furniture manufacturer to produce chairs. When the prices of these and other products indicate that consumers value them as much or more than their production costs, producers seeking personal gain will supply them.

Nor will it be necessary for anyone to remind producers to search for and utilize low-cost methods of production. Self-interest directed by the invisible hand of market prices will provide them with an incentive to seek out the best combination of resources and the most cost-effective

---

7. F. A. Hayek, "The Use of Knowledge in Society," *American Economic Review* 35 (September 1945): 519–30.

production methods. Because lower costs will mean higher profits, each producer will strive to keep costs down and quality up. In fact, competition will virtually force them to do so.

In a modern economy, the cooperation that comes from self-interest directed by the invisible hand of market prices is truly amazing. The next time you sit down to a nice dinner, think about all the people who helped make it possible. It is unlikely that any of them—from the farmer to the truck driver to the grocer—was motivated by concern that you have an enjoyable meal at the lowest possible cost. Market prices, however, brought their interests into harmony with yours. Farmers who raise the best beef or turkeys receive higher prices, truck drivers and grocers earn more money if their products are delivered fresh and in good condition to the consumer, and so on, always using the low-cost means to do so. Literally tens of thousands of people, most of whom we will never meet, make contributions that help each of us consume a bundle of goods that is far greater than what we could produce for ourselves. Moreover, the invisible hand works so quietly and automatically that the order, cooperation, and availability of a vast array of goods and services are largely taken for granted. Even though underappreciated, the combination of self-interest and the invisible hand is nonetheless a powerful force for economic progress.

12. *Too often long-term consequences, or the secondary effects, of an action are ignored.*

In 1946, Henry Hazlitt, a famous economic journalist, wrote a book titled *Economics in One Lesson*. This economics primer, which builds on an 1850 essay by the Frenchman Frédéric Bastiat (who was also an economic journalist), is perhaps the all-time bestselling treatise in economics.

The book starts with the story of a young boy who breaks the window of a shopkeeper by throwing a ball through it. As a result, the shopkeeper hires a glazer to fix the window. Some observers, noting the highly visible employment of the glazer, argue that the broken window is a good thing because it created a job for the glazer. However, as Hazlitt stresses, this is wrong because it ignores the secondary effects.

If the shopkeeper had not spent the funds fixing the window, he would have spent them on other things, perhaps a pair of shoes, new clothes, or similar items. If the window had not been broken, employment in these other areas of production would have been larger and the community would have had both the window and the items purchased by the shopkeeper. Once the secondary effects are considered, it is clear that destructive actions such as those resulting from floods, hurricanes, and destructive public policy harm a society and fail to expand net employment. The view that destructive acts create employment and are good for the economy is now known as the "broken window fallacy." See Element 9 above for several examples of this fallacious view.

Hazlitt's one lesson was that when analyzing an economic proposal, a person:

> . . . *must trace not merely the immediate results but the results in the long run, not merely the primary consequences but the secondary consequences, and not merely the effects on some special group but the effects on everyone.*[8]

Hazlitt believed that failure to apply this lesson was the most common source of economic error. He had written extensively on the economy during the Great Depression of the 1930s, and he knew that, especially in politics, there is a tendency to stress the short-term benefits of a policy while ignoring the longer-term often unintended consequences.

Let's consider a couple of examples that illustrate the potential

8. Henry Hazlitt, *Economics in One Lesson* (New Rochelle: Arlington House, 1979): 103.

importance of secondary effects. In an effort to reduce gasoline consumption, the federal government mandates that automobiles be more fuel efficient. Is this regulation a sound policy? It may be, but when evaluating the policy's overall impact, one should look at the unintended secondary effects.

To achieve the higher fuel efficiency, auto manufacturers reduced the size and weight of vehicles. As a result, there are more highway deaths— about 2,500 more per year—than would otherwise occur because these lighter cars do not offer as much protection for occupants. Furthermore, because the higher mileage standards for cars and light trucks make driving cheaper, people tend to drive more than they otherwise would. This increases congestion and results in a smaller reduction in gasoline consumption than was intended by the regulation. Once you consider the secondary effects, the fuel efficiency regulations are much less beneficial than they might first appear.

Trade restrictions between nations have important secondary effects as well. The proponents of **tariffs** and **import quotas** on foreign goods almost always ignore the secondary effects of their policies. Tariffs and quotas may initially protect the U.S. workers who make similar products at a higher cost. But there will be unintended secondary consequences.

Consider the import quotas restricting the sale of foreign-produced sugar in the United States. As the result of these quotas, for many years the domestic price of sugar in the United States has been approximately twice the price in the rest of the world. The proponents of this policy— primarily sugar producers—argue that the quotas "save jobs" and increase employment. No doubt, the employment of sugar growers in the United States is higher than it otherwise would be. But what about the secondary effects?

The higher sugar prices mean it's more expensive for U.S. firms to produce candy and other products that use a lot of sugar. As a result, many candy producers, including the makers of Life Savers, Jaw Breakers, Red Huts, Fannie May and Fanny Farmer chocolates, and Oreo cookies have moved to countries like Canada and Mexico, where sugar can be purchased at its true market price. Thus, employment among sugar-using firms in the United States is lower than it otherwise would be. Further, because foreigners sell less sugar in the United States, they have less purchasing power with which to buy products we export to them. This, too, reduces U.S. employment.

Once the secondary effects of trade restrictions like the sugar quota program are taken into consideration, there is no reason to expect U.S. employment to increase as a result. There may be more jobs in favored industries, but there will be less employment in others. Trade restrictions reshuffle employment rather than increase it. But those who fail to consider the secondary effects will miss this point. Clearly, consideration of the secondary effects is an important ingredient of the economic way of thinking.

Secondary effects are not just a problem with political decision-making. They can also lead to unanticipated outcomes for individuals. The recent experience of a first grade teacher in West Virginia illustrates this point. Her students were constantly losing their pencils; so she reasoned that if she paid them 10 cents for the stub they would respond to the incentive to hang on to the pencil until it was all used. To her dismay, the students soon formed long lines at the pencil sharpener, creating stubs just as fast as she could pay for them. It pays to be alert for unintended consequences!

PART 2

*Seven Major Sources
of Economic Progress*

SEVEN MAJOR SOURCES OF ECONOMIC PROGRESS

1. Legal system: The foundation for economic progress is a legal system that protects privately owned property and enforces contracts in an evenhanded manner.

2. Competitive markets: Competition promotes the efficient use of resources and provides the incentive for innovative improvements.

3. Limits on government regulation: Regulatory policies that reduce exchange and restrict competition impede economic progress.

4. An efficient capital market: To realize its potential, a nation must have a mechanism that channels capital into wealth-creating projects.

5. Monetary stability: A stable monetary policy is essential for the control of inflation, efficient allocation of investment, and achievement of economic stability.

6. Low tax rates: People produce more when they can keep more of what they earn.

7. Free trade: People achieve higher incomes when they are free to trade with people in other countries.

Introduction

Robert Lucas, the 1995 Nobel Laureate, stated, "Once you start thinking about economic growth, it is hard to think about anything else."[1] Why do Lucas and many other economists place so much emphasis on economic growth? Growth of real output is necessary for the growth of real income. Without growth, higher income levels and living standards cannot be achieved.

During the past two hundred years, economic growth, particularly in the West, has elevated living standards and improved both the length and quality of life. This period, however, is exceptional. Throughout most of human history, economic growth has been extremely rare. Prior to 1800, most of the world's population worked hard for fifty, sixty, and seventy hours per week in order to obtain enough food and shelter for subsistence. It was a constant struggle for survival and many lost the battle. Living standards in 1800 were not much different than a thousand years earlier, or even two thousand years earlier during the time of ancient Rome.

---

1. See Robert E. Lucas Jr., "On the Mechanics of Economic Development," *Journal of Monetary Economics* 22, No. 1 (1988): 3–42.

The bleak economic story of human history began to change about two hundred years ago. The late Angus Maddison, an economist for the Organisation for Economic Co-operation and Development, is widely recognized as the leading authority on historical income and life expectancy data. Exhibit 4 presents his estimated annual income levels per person for the past thousand years. Measured in 1990 dollars, the **gross domestic product (GDP)** per person of the world was $667 in 1820, compared to $450 in 1000.[2] Thus, over 800 years, per-person income levels increased by only about 50 percent. Western Europe and its offshoots of the United States, Canada, Australia, and New Zealand—commonly referred to as the West—did a little better, as income in this region approximately tripled from $426 in 1000 to $1,202 in 1820. But even in the West it took around five hundred years for income to double.

Now, take a good look at what has happened since 1820. During the past two hundred years, there has been a virtual explosion of economic growth. By 2003, the world's income per person had risen to $6,516, ten times the level of 1820. In the West, by 2003 income per person had soared to $23,710, nearly twenty times the figure for 1820. Thus, after experiencing centuries of income levels at or near subsistence, real per capita income has skyrocketed during the past two hundred years.

The pattern of life expectancy was similar. Life expectancy at birth for the world rose from 24 years to 26 years between 1000 and 1820, but it then increased to 31 years in 1900 before soaring to 64 years in 2003. In the West, life expectancy rose from 24 years to 36 years between 1000 and 1820, but by 2003 it had reached 76 years.

As history illustrates, economic growth does not occur automati-

2. The most widely used measure of total output and income is gross domestic product (GDP). Changes in GDP are also widely used to measure the growth of an economy. For more information on GDP, see supplementary reading "Gross Domestic Product (GDP): What Is It and How Is It Measured?" at the website accompanying this book: Common SenseEconomics.com/wp-content/uploads/CSE_GDP_Student.pdf.

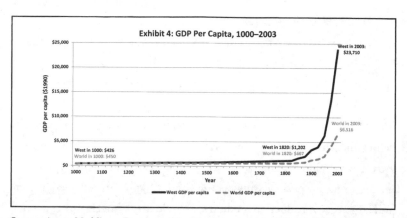

Source: Angus Maddison, Contours of the World Economy, 1–2030AD: *Essays in Macro-Economic History* (Oxford: Oxford University Press, 2007).

cally. Why do some countries grow and achieve high levels of income while others stagnate? What institutions and policies will promote growth and higher living standards? This section examines these vitally important questions.[3]

1. Legal system: *The foundation for economic progress is a legal system that protects privately owned property and enforces contracts in an evenhanded manner.*

[A] private property regime makes people responsible for their own actions in the realm of material goods. Such a system therefore

3. While a diverse set of factors influences growth and development, the modern view recognizes the central role of institutions and policies. Leading contributors to the modern view include Nobel Laureate Douglass North, English economist Peter Bauer, Daron Acemoglu of the Massachusetts Institute of Technology, and James Robinson of Harvard. See Peter T. Bauer, *Dissent on Development: Studies and Debates in Development Economics* (Cambridge: Harvard University Press, 1972); D.C. North, *Institutions, Institutional Change, and Economic Performance* (Cambridge: Cambridge University Press, 1990) and; Daron Acemoglu and James A. Robinson, *Why Nations Fail: The Origins of Power, Prosperity, and Poverty* (New York: Crown, 2012).

ensures that people experience the consequences of their own acts. Property sets up fences, but it also surrounds us with mirrors, reflecting back upon us the consequences of our own behaviour.[4]

—Tom Bethell, Economic Journalist

The legal system provides the foundation for the protection of property rights and enforcement of contracts. As we discussed in Element 4 of Part 1, trade moves goods toward people who value them more and makes larger outputs possible as the result of gains from specialization and large-scale production methods. To reduce the uncertainties accompanying trade, a legal system must provide evenhanded enforcement of agreements and contracts. This increases the volume of exchange and the gains from trade, and thereby promotes economic progress.

Well-defined and enforced property rights are crucial for the realization of gains from trade. Property is a broad term that includes ownership of labor services, as well as physical assets such as buildings and land. Private ownership of property involves three things: (1) the right to exclusive use; (2) legal protection against invaders—those who would seek to use or abuse the property without the owner's permission; and (3) the right to transfer (sell or give) to others.

Private owners can decide how they will use their property, but they are held accountable for their actions. People who use their property in a manner that invades or infringes on the property rights of another will be subject to the same legal forces that protect their own property. For example, **private property rights** prohibit me from throwing my hammer through the windshield of your automobile because if I did, I would be violating your property right to your car. Your property right to your automobile restricts me and everyone else from its use (or abuse) without your permission. Similarly, my ownership of my hammer and other pos-

4. Tom Bethell, *The Noblest Triumph* (New York: St. Martin's Press, 1998): 10.

restricts you and everyone else from using them without my permission.

The important thing about private ownership is the incentives that flow from it. There are four major reasons why the incentives accompanying clearly defined and enforced private ownership rights propel economic growth and progress.

First, private ownership provides people with a strong incentive to maintain and care for items that they own. If private owners fail to maintain their property or if they allow it to be abused or damaged, they will bear the consequences in the form of a decline in their property's value. For example, if you own an automobile, you have a strong incentive to change the oil, have the car serviced regularly, and see that the interior of the car is well-maintained. Why is this so? If you are careless in these areas, the car's value to both you and potential future owners will decline. If the car is kept in good running order, it will be of greater value to you and to others who might want to buy it from you. For the owner, the market price will reflect that stewardship. Good stewardship is rewarded, but bad stewardship is penalized by a reduction in the value of the asset.

In contrast, when property is owned by the government or owned in common by a large group of people, the incentive for each user to take good care of it is weakened. For example, when the government owns housing, no individual or small group of owners has a strong financial incentive to maintain the property, because no individual or small group will pay the costs of a decline in the value of the property or benefit from its improvement. That is why government-owned housing, compared to privately owned housing, is more often run down and poorly maintained. This is true in both capitalist nations where markets provide price signals, and in socialist countries where they do not. Laxity in care, maintenance, and repair reflects the weak incentives that accompany government ownership of property, even in the midst of working markets for other privately owned assets.

Second, private ownership encourages people to use and develop their property in ways others value highly. If they employ and develop their property in ways that others find attractive, the market value of the property will increase. In contrast, changes that others dislike—particularly if the others are customers or potential future buyers—will reduce the value of one's property.

Private ownership also affects personal development. When people are able to keep the fruits of their labor, they have a powerful incentive to improve their skills, work harder, and work smarter. Such actions will increase their income. Why are college students willing to endure long hours of study and incur the cost of a college education? Private ownership of labor services provides the answer. Because they have an ownership right to their labor services, their future earnings will be higher if they acquire knowledge and develop skills that are highly valued by others.

Similarly, private ownership provides the owners of land, buildings, and other physical assets with an incentive to use, protect, and develop them in ways that are beneficial to others. Further, those who fail to do so will bear the cost in terms of a lower value of their assets. Consider the owner of an apartment complex who personally cares nothing about having parking spaces, convenient laundry facilities, a nice workout room, or an attractive lawn and swimming pool within the complex. If consumers value these things highly (relative to the costs of producing them), the apartment owner has a strong incentive to provide them. Why? Consumers will be willing to pay higher rents for apartments with the highly valued amenities. Thus, apartment owners who supply such amenities will be able to improve the well-being of their customers and increase their own net earnings (and the market value of their apartment complex). In contrast, apartment owners who insist on providing only what they like, rather than the things that consumers prefer, will find that their earnings and the value of their capital (their apartments) will decline.

Interestingly, private ownership influences productivity even in socialist countries. Farming in the former Soviet Union illustrates this
point. Under the Communist regime, families were permitted to keep or
sell the goods they produced on small private plots, which ranged up to
an acre in size. These private plots made up only about 2 percent of the
total land under cultivation; the other 98 percent consisted of huge, collectively owned farms where the land and the output belonged to the
state. As reported by the Soviet press, approximately one-fourth of the
total value of Soviet agricultural output was raised on that tiny fraction
of privately farmed land. This indicates that the output per acre on the
private plots was about sixteen times that of the state-owned farms.

Even a modest move away from state ownership toward private
ownership can produce impressive results. In 1978 the Communist government of China began a de facto policy of letting farmers keep all rice
grown on the collective farms over and above a specified grain quota that
had to be given to the state. The result was an immediate increase in
productivity because farmers had an incentive to produce efficiently.
Once the quotas were met, the farmers were permitted to keep all of their
additional output. When the word got out and the government ignored
the official policy against such "privatization," the practice spread like
wildfire, leading to rapid increases in agricultural output and freeing
farmers to move into nonagricultural sectors of the economy.[5]

Third, private ownership makes owners legally responsible for damages imposed on others as the result of how their property is used. Courts
of law recognize and enforce the authority granted by ownership, but
they also enforce the responsibility that goes with that authority. Private

---

5. For additional information, see John McMillan, *Reinventing the Bazaar: A Natural
History of Markets* (New York: W. W. Norton, 2002): 94–101. As McMillan points out,
real privatization would have been preferred. Nonetheless, the movement toward private
ownership was still "the biggest anti-poverty program the world has ever seen." (See
page 94.)

ownership links control with responsibility. Owners are held responsible precisely because they are in a position to exercise control. In turn, this accountability provides owners with a strong incentive to use their property responsibly and take steps to reduce the likelihood of harm to others.

Consider the following examples. The owner of a dying tree has an incentive to cut it down before it falls into a neighbor's house. Dog owners have an incentive to leash or restrain their dogs if they are likely to bite others. A car owner has a right to drive his car, but will be held accountable if the brakes aren't maintained and the car damages someone else's property. Similarly, a chemical company has control over its products, but, exactly for that reason, it is legally liable for damages if it mishandles the chemicals.

Fourth, private ownership promotes the conservation of resources for the future, as well as wise development. Using a resource may generate revenue, which reflects the desires of present consumers who want what the resource can provide. But future consumers also have a voice, thanks to property rights. An owner of a resource, say a woodlot or small forest whose trees could be harvested now or later, faces a decision. Will the timber be more valuable later? In other words, will the expected value of the trees when they are more mature be greater than if they are logged today? And will that value exceed their value if harvested now by more than the cost of holding and protecting them for future use? If so, the owner has an incentive to conserve—that is, hold back on current use—to make sure that the resource will be available when it is more valuable.

Private owners will gain by conservation whenever the future value of a consumable resource is expected to exceed its current value. This is true even if the current owner does not expect to be around when the benefits accrue. Suppose a sixty-five-year-old tree farmer plants a crop of Douglas fir trees that typically take fifty years to grow to their optimal harvesting level. Does the elderly tree farmer have an incentive to conserve the trees for future use? With private ownership rights, the answer is clearly "yes." As long as the growth of the trees is expected to enhance future revenue as much as alternative investments would, the farmer will gain by conserving the trees for the future. With private ownership, the market value of the farmer's land will increase as the trees grow and the expected day of harvest moves closer. So even though actual logging may not take place until well after his death, the owner will be able to sell the trees (or the land including the trees) at any time, capturing their increasing value.

For centuries pessimists have argued that we are about to run out of trees, critical minerals, or various sources of energy. Again and again, they have been wrong because they failed to recognize the role of private property. It is instructive to reflect on these doomsday forecasts. In sixteenth-century England fear arose that the supply of wood—widely used as heating fuel—would soon be exhausted. Higher wood prices, however, encouraged conservation and led to the development of coal. The wood crisis soon dissipated.

Even when a specific resource is not owned, the market for other resources that are owned can often solve problems. In the middle of the nineteenth century, dire predictions arose that the United States was about to run out of whale oil, the primary fuel for artificial lighting at the time. No one owned the whales, which were being hunted to excess on the high seas. If a whale hunter failed to take a whale when the opportunity arose, someone else would probably do so in the near future. As whale oil prices rose, the incentive for individuals to conserve whales for the future was missing because private ownership rights were absent. No one limited whale hunting even though the whale population was declining.

However, the higher whale oil prices strengthened the incentive to find and develop substitute energy sources. If entrepreneurs could develop a cheaper new energy source, they could earn substantial revenues. With time, this led to the discovery of commercially profitable sources of petroleum, the development of relatively cheaper kerosene, a resulting drop in the price of whale oil, less whale hunting, and thus the end of the whale oil crisis.

Later, as people switched to petroleum, predictions emerged that this resource, too, would be exhausted. In 1914 the Bureau of Mines reported that the total U.S. supply of oil was under six billion barrels, about what the United States now produces every forty months. In 1926 the Federal Oil Conservation Board estimated that the U.S. supply of oil would last only for another seven years. More recently, a study sponsored by the highly influencial Club of Rome made similar predictions for the world during the 1970s.

Understanding the incentives that emanate from private ownership makes it easy to see why doomsday forecasts have been so wrong. When the scarcity of a privately owned resource increases, the price of the resource will rise. The increase in price provides consumers, producers, innovators, and engineers with incentives to (1) conserve on the direct use of the resource; (2) search more diligently for **substitutes**; and (3) develop new methods of discovering and recovering larger amounts of the resource. To date, these forces have pushed doomsday ever further into the future, and there is every reason to believe that they will continue to do so for resources that are privately owned.[6]

A legal system that protects property rights and enforces contracts

6. There have been cases where humans have hunted an animal species to extinction. Passenger pigeons are an example. They were hunted for meat while whales were hunted mainly for oil. But pigeons were such a small part of the market for meat that even as they began to disappear, the price of meat did not increase enough to call forth either preservation efforts or a large-scale increase in the production of meats. There was no crisis. So their disappearance became complete. If whales had been intensively hunted only for their meat, and not mainly for oil, they also might have disappeared. But whale oil was so important in the market for light that when its price rose sharply, a substitute was found that reduced the demand for whale oil and its price, saving the whales.

in an evenhanded manner provides the foundation for gains from trade, **capital formation,** and resource development, which comprise the mainsprings of economic growth. In contrast, insecure property rights, uncertain enforcement of agreements, and legal favoritism undermine both investment and the productive use of resources. Throughout history people have tried other forms of ownership such as large-scale cooperatives, socialism, and communism. On any scale beyond the small village with a strong cultural harmony, these experiences have ranged from unsuccessful to disastrous. To date, we do not know of any institutional arrangement that provides individuals with as much freedom and incentive to serve others by using resources productively and efficiently as does private ownership within the framework of the **rule of law.**

2. *Competitive markets: Competition promotes the efficient use of resources and provides the incentive for innovative improvements.*

> *Competition is conducive to the continuous improvements of industrial efficiency. It leads producers to eliminate wastes and cut costs so that they may undersell others. It weeds out those whose costs remain high and thus operates to concentrate production in the hands of those whose costs are low.*[7]
>
> —CLAIR WILCOX, FORMER PROFESSOR
> OF ECONOMICS, SWARTHMORE COLLEGE

Competition is present when the market is open and alternative sellers are free to enter. Competition is the lifeblood of a market economy. The

---

7. Clair Wilcox, *Competition and Monopoly in American Industry*. Monograph No. 21, Temporary National Economic Committee, Investigation of Concentration of Economic Power, 76th Cong. 3d sess. (Washington, D.C.: U.S. Government Printing Office, 1940).

rival firms may operate in local, regional, national, or even global markets. The competitive process places pressure on each to operate efficiently and cater to the preferences of consumers. Competition weeds out inefficient producers. Firms that fail to provide consumers with quality goods at attractive prices will experience losses and eventually be driven out of business. Successful competitors have to outperform rival firms. They may do so through a variety of methods, including quality of product, style, service, convenience of location, advertising, and price, but they must consistently offer consumers at least as much value relative to cost as is available from rivals.

What keeps McDonald's, Walmart, Amazon, General Motors, or any other business firm from raising prices, selling shoddy products, and providing lousy service? Competition provides the answer. If McDonald's fails to provide a tasty sandwich at an attractive price delivered with a smile, people will turn to Burger King, Wendy's, Subway, Taco Bell, and other rivals. Even the largest firms will lose business to small upstarts that find ways to provide consumers with better products at lower prices. For example, when Walmart was nothing more than a few small stores in Arkansas, Sears was a retailing giant. Now, Walmart is the world's largest retailer with sales that dwarf those of Sears. Firms as large as Toyota, General Motors, and Ford will lose customers to Honda, Hyundai, Volkswagen, and other automobile manufacturers if they fall even a step behind in providing the type of vehicle people want at competitive prices.

Competition gives firms a strong incentive to develop better products and discover lower-cost methods of production. Because technology and prices change constantly, no one knows precisely what products consumers will want next or which production techniques will minimize costs per unit. Competition helps discover the answer. Is marketing through social media the greatest retail idea since the shopping mall? Or is it simply another dream that will eventually turn to vapor? Competition will provide the answer, which will differ across markets and change over time.

In a market economy entrepreneurs are free to innovate. They need only the support of investors (often including themselves) willing to put up the necessary funds. The approval of central planners, a legislative majority, or business rivals is not required. Nonetheless, competition holds entrepreneurs and the investors who support them accountable because their ideas must face a "reality check" imposed by consumers. If consumers value the innovation enough to cover its costs, the new business will profit and prosper. But if consumers find that the new product is worth less than it costs, the business will suffer losses and fail. Consumers are the ultimate judge and jury of business innovation and performance.

When new products are introduced, they typically follow a predictable price-quality pattern. Initially, new products are generally very expensive and purchased by relatively few consumers, mostly those with high incomes. These consumers will pay dearly for the earlier availability because during this initial phase, the product quality will be low and the price high. These initial purchasers play a vital role: They provide the revenue to cover the product's start-up cost and make it possible for entrepreneurs to acquire the experience that will help them improve quality and reduce per-unit cost in the future. Moreover, market incentives will encourage them to do so. With time, entrepreneurs will figure out how to make the product more affordable and expand its availability to more and more consumers. The cellular phone illustrates this price-quality pattern. When cell phones were initially introduced in the late 1980s, they sold for around $4,000, were about the size of a brick, and could not do much of anything other than make phone calls. With time, their size was reduced, their information processing power and functions expanded, and their price declined. Today, they are available at a fraction of the initial price and they are viewed as a necessity by many consumers in all income brackets. Numerous goods, including automobiles, televisions, air conditioners, dishwashers, microwave ovens, and personal computers have gone through this same pattern. All were highly expensive when they were initially introduced, but entrepreneurs figured out how to produce them more economically and improve their quality, making them more affordable to the overwhelming bulk of consumers. As we reflect on the role of both entrepreneurs and the competitive process, it is important to recognize this price-quality pattern.

Producers who wish to survive in a competitive environment cannot be complacent. Today's successful product may not pass tomorrow's competitive test. In order to succeed in a competitive market, entrepreneurs must be good at anticipating, identifying, and quickly adopting improved ideas.

Competition also discovers the business structure and size of firm that can best keep the per-unit cost of a product or service low. Unlike other economic systems, a market economy does not mandate the types of firms that are permitted to compete. Any form of business organization is permissible. An owner-operated firm, partnership, corporation, employee-owned firm, consumer cooperative, commune, or any other form of business is free to enter the market. To succeed it has to pass only one test: cost-effectiveness. If a business entity, whether a corporation or an employee-owned firm, produces quality products at attractive prices, it will profit and succeed. But if its structure results in higher costs than other forms of business organization, competition will drive it from the market.

The competitive process will also determine the size of firms in various sectors of the economy. In some sectors—the manufacturing of airplanes and automobiles, for example—firms will need to be quite large to take full advantage of economies of scale. Building a single automobile would be extremely costly, but when the fixed costs are spread over many thousands of units, the costs of producing each car can plummet. Naturally, consumers will tend to buy from the firms that can produce goods economically and sell them at lower prices. In such industries, small firms will be unable to compete effectively and only large firms will survive.

In other sectors, however, small firms, often organized as individual proprietorships or partnerships, will be more cost-effective. When consumers place a high value on personalized service and individualized products, small firms will tend to dominate and large firms will have difficulty competing. This is generally the case in the markets for legal and medical services, gourmet restaurants, hair styling, and specialized printing. Thus, these markets are usually dominated by small firms.

Paradoxical as it may seem, self-interest directed by competition is a powerful force for economic progress. Dynamic competition among products, technologies, organizational methods, and business firms will weed out the inefficient and consistently lead to the discovery and introduction of superior products and technologies. When the new methods improve quality and/or reduce costs, they will grow rapidly and often replace the old ways of doing things.

History abounds with examples. The automobile replaces the horse and buggy. The supermarket replaces the mom-and-pop grocery store. Fast-food chains like McDonald's and Wendy's largely replace the local diner. Walmart and Target grow rapidly while other retailers contract, and firms like Montgomery Ward and Kmart are driven from the market. MP3s and iPods replace CD players, which had previously displaced cassette decks and record players. Personal computers replace typewriters, and smart phones substitute for less mobile computer devices. One could go on and on with similar examples. The great economist Joseph Schumpeter referred to this dynamic competition as "creative destruction," and he argued that it formed the very core of economic progress.

Competition harnesses personal self-interest and puts it to work, elevating our society's standard of living. As Adam Smith noted in *The Wealth of Nations:*

It is not from the benevolence of the butcher, the brewer, or the baker that we expect our dinner, but from their regard to their own self-interest. We address ourselves not to their humanity but to their self-love, and never talk to them of our own necessities, but of their advantages.[8]

Taken together, private ownership and competitive markets provide the foundation for cooperative behavior and efficient use of resources. When private property rights are clearly defined and enforced, producers face the opportunity cost of their resource use. At the same time, prices in open and competitive markets provide producers with a strong incentive to keep cost low, cater to the desires of consumers, and discover superior products and better ways of doing things.

It is important to note that competition is not "pro-business." In fact, businesses do not like to face competition and they commonly lobby for policies to protect themselves from it. They will often seek to erect barriers limiting the market entry of potential rivals. As we move on to the analysis of regulation and the political process, examples of business behavior seeking to reduce the competitiveness of markets will arise again and again.

3. Limits on government regulation: Regulatory policies that reduce exchange and restrict competition impede economic progress.

As we previously noted, gains from trade directed by competitive markets promote both economic progress and social cooperation. Government regulations, often promoted by established businesses, are

8. Adam Smith. *An Inquiry into the Nature and Causes of the Wealth of Nations,* Volume I Glasgow Edition (Indianapolis: Liberty Fund, Inc., [1776] 1981): 18. Also available at: www.econlib.org/library/Smith/smWN.html.

a major source of trade barriers and market entry restraints. There are three major ways that regulations limit exchange and reduce the competitiveness of markets.

First, regulations often restrict entry into markets. Many countries impose regulations that make it difficult to enter and compete in various businesses and occupations. In those countries, if you want to start a business or provide a service, you have to acquire a license, fill out forms, get permission from different bureaus, show that you are qualified, indicate that you have sufficient financing, and meet various other regulatory tests. Some officials may refuse your application unless you are willing to pay a bribe or contribute to their political coffers. Often, well-established and politically influential businesses that you would be competing against can successfully oppose your application.

Hernando de Soto, in his revealing book *The Mystery of Capital,* reports that in Lima, Peru, it took 289 days for a team of people working six hours a day to meet the regulations required to legally open a small business producing garments. (In an earlier book, *The Other Path,* he revealed that along the way, ten bribes were solicited and it was necessary to pay two of the requested bribes in order to get permission to operate legally.) The World Bank reports that, given the regulations in place in 2015, legally opening a business would take 97 days in Haiti, 119 days in Brazil, and 144 days in Venezuela. By way of comparison, opening this same business would take only 2.5 days in Hong Kong or Singapore and 4 days in the United States.[9]

Second, regulations that substitute political authority for the rule of law and freedom of contract will tend to undermine gains from trade. Several countries make a habit of adopting laws that grant political administrators substantial discretionary authority. For example, in the

---

9. World Bank, *Doing Business Project, 2015.* Available at *Doing Business Project,* World Bank Group, n.d. www.doingbusiness.org/data/.

mid-1980s customs officials in Guatemala were permitted to waive tariffs if they thought that doing so was in the "national interest." Such legislation is an open invitation for government officials to solicit bribes. It creates regulatory uncertainty and makes business activity costlier and less attractive, particularly for honest people. Popular support for regulation often stems from the desire to promote a cleaner environment or provide consumers with protection against unscrupulous business operators. Regulations can play a positive role in these areas. Even here, however, the law needs to be precise, unambiguous, and nondiscriminatory. If it is not, it will be a roadblock to gains from trade.

Regulations often help some businesses by restricting competitors. Because such regulations are lucrative to the few who benefit, they impose an additional cost: Businesses, labor organizations, and other special-interest groups will seek advantage for their constituents by trying to influence the political process. Some will lobby politicians and regulators to establish or increase these roadblocks, while others (those most severely harmed) will lobby to diminish their effects. Lobbying for all sides of any issue consumes the time and effort of highly skilled individuals who could be producing wealth instead of seeking political advantages from policies that reduce the productivity of others.

Third, the imposition of price controls will also stifle trade. Governments sometimes set prices above the market level. For example, some governments require that the producers of various agricultural products be paid a specified minimum price for their commodities. At the higher set price, buyers will purchase fewer units than they otherwise would. Governments also set prices lower than the market level, as in cases of apartment rent controls and regulated electric power rates. In terms of units produced and sold, it makes little difference whether price controls push prices up or force them down; both will reduce the volume of trade and the gains from production and exchange.

Minimum wage rates are perhaps the most commonly imposed price control throughout the world. A minimum wage rate establishes a price floor that pushes the hourly wage of some workers (and jobs) above the market level. It is currently a hot topic in the United States. Several leaders of both major political parties have called for a higher federal minimum wage. Moreover, several cities including Seattle, San Francisco, and Los Angeles recently adopted $15 per hour minimum wage rates.

The basic postulate of economics indicates that a higher minimum wage will reduce the employment of low-skill workers. There is some controversy about the size of the employment reduction, but the weight of the empirical evidence indicates that each 10 percent increase in the minimum wage will reduce employment by between 1 and 2 percent. Because the wage increases are substantially larger than the reductions in employment, a higher minimum wage will nearly always increase the total earnings of low-skill workers. The proponents of higher minimum wages believe that the higher total earnings are well worth the cost of the relatively small reductions in employment.

Many supporters of a higher minimum wage also believe that it will reduce the poverty rate. At first glance, this appears to be true, but examination of the data indicates it is highly questionable. There are three major reasons why this is the case. First, the bulk of minimum wage employees—about 80 percent—are members of households with incomes above the poverty level; one-third live in households with above-average incomes. Half of the minimum wage workers are between the ages of 16 and 24 years and most of these work part-time. Only one out of every seven minimum wage workers (about 15 percent) is the primary earner for a family with one or more children. Thus, the typical minimum wage worker is a single, youthful, part-time secondary worker in a household with an income above the poverty level. Second, there will be unintended effects of the higher minimum. Employers will take steps to control (or compensate for) their higher wage costs. These will include a reduction in hours worked, fewer training opportunities, a less convenient work schedule, and fewer fringe benefits. Further, many of the minimum wage workers are also consumers of products impacted by the higher minimum wage. These workers will have to pay higher prices for goods such as fast food. Thus, the actual compensation of the minimum wage workers will increase by less than the expansion in the minimum.[10] Finally, more than half of the poor families in the United States do not have anyone in the labor force, and therefore a higher minimum wage will not help them. The data presented here are from government sources and widely accepted by professional economists.

When thinking about the effects of the minimum wage on youthful low-skill workers, it is important to consider the impact in both the short and long run. Work experience provides youthful workers with an opportunity to develop self-confidence, good work habits, and skills and attitudes that will make them more valuable to future employers. This opportunity is particularly important for high school dropouts and others with weak educational backgrounds. Unless these young people are able to prove their value to employers and develop on-the-job skills, it is unlikely that they will be able to move up the job ladder and realize higher earnings in the future.

The value of work experience and skill development is widely recognized in the case of those with higher levels of education. For example, college students often take unpaid internships—that is, they work for a zero wage—with government agencies and nonprofit organizations in order to gain experience that will enhance their future earning opportunities. Indeed, members of Congress advertise unpaid internships to college students by pointing out the benefits of work experience in beginning-level jobs. Yet many of these same politicians support minimum wage levels that reduce the opportunity of disadvantaged youth to

10. For a comprehensive analysis of the impact of minimum wage legislation on the poor, see Thomas MaCurdy, "How Effective Is the Minimum Wage at Supporting the Poor?" *Journal of Political Economy* 123 (2015): 2.www.jstor.org/stable/full/10.1086/679626.

acquire the work experience and on-the-job training that will enhance their future employment prospects. This adverse impact on low-skill youth is almost always ignored, except by economists. Nonetheless, it is an important unintended secondary effect of minimum wages that adversely impacts the long-term employment of young people, particularly those with the least amount of education.

Regulations are particularly important in labor markets. Many countries have imposed regulations that interfere with and undermine the use of contracts or voluntary agreements to deal with various issues. Dismissal regulations provide an example. A number of European countries require employers who want to reduce the size of their workforce to (1) obtain permission from political authorities; (2) notify the dismissed employees months in advance; and (3) continue paying the dismissed employees for several more months.

Such regulations may appear to be in the interests of workers, but the secondary effects must be considered. Regulations that make it costly to dismiss workers also make it costly to hire them; employers will be reluctant to take on additional workers because of the high dismissal costs. As a result, it will be difficult for new labor force entrants to find jobs, and the growth of employment will be slowed. This has been the case in European countries, where restrictive labor market regulations are more pronounced than in the United States. Such regulations are a major reason why the unemployment rates of Western European countries such as Italy, Spain, and France have been 4 or 5 percentage points higher than the United States during the past couple of decades.[11]

While hiring and dismissal regulations are generally less restrictive in the United States than in Europe, occupational licensing is a major

---

11. For evidence on this point, see Edward Bierhanzl and James Gwartney, "Regulation, Unions, and Labor Markets," *Regulation* (Summer 1998): 40–53.

labor market restriction in the United States. Most of the occupational licensing occurs at the state level. In order to obtain a license, one has to pay fees ranging from modest to exorbitant, take training courses for 6 to 12 months, and pass examinations.

As recently as 1970, fewer than 15 percent of Americans worked in jobs that required a license. Today, the figure is nearly 30 percent, and it is continuing to grow. In the mid-1980s, 800 occupations were licensed in at least one state; now, according to the Council on Licensure, Enforcement and Regulation, more than 1,100 occupations are licensed.

The supporters of licensing argue that it is necessary to protect consumers from shoddy and potentially unsafe products. But, licenses are required in numerous occupations that have little to do with public safety or protection of the consumer.[12] For example, one or more states require a person to be licensed in order to work in the following occupations: interior designer, makeup artist, florist, hair braider, shampoo specialist, dietician, private detective, athletic trainer, tour guide, hearing-aid fitter, funeral attendant, casket seller, and even a ferret breeder and a palm reader. The pressure for licensing seldom originates from consumer groups. Instead, it nearly always arises from those already in the occupation. This is not surprising to economists because the current suppliers are the primary beneficiaries of licensing.

Individuals can often acquire the skills necessary for high-level performance in many licensed occupations through on-the-job experience and working with others skilled in the trade. The licensing requirements prohibit persons developing their skills via these methods from pursuing their desired career. Licensing, particularly when it mandates lengthy

12. See the Department of Treasury, Office of Economic Policy, *Occupational Licensing: A Framework for Policymakers,* 2015; Morris M. Kleiner, "Why License a Florist?" *New York Times,* May 28, 2014; Jacob Goldstein, "So You Think You Can Be a Hair Braider?" *New York Times,* June 12, 2012; and Dick M. Carpenter II, Lisa Knepper, Angela C. Erickson, and John K. Ross, *License to Work: A National Study of Burdens from Occupational Licensing,* Institute for Justice, May 2012.

formal training and levies expensive fees, reduces supply and drives up the price of the goods and services provided by the licensed practitioners. Those currently in the occupation gain at the expense of consumers and unlicensed potential producers. The employment opportunities of the unlicensed producers are diminished and potential gains from trade lost.

Certification provides an attractive alternative to licensing. With certification, the government could require suppliers to provide information about their education, training, and other qualifications to consumers, without prohibiting anyone from working in his or her chosen field. In essence, certification makes information about the suppliers' qualifications readily available to consumers, without restricting their choices. Further, it would make it possible for practitioners to develop and demonstrate their competence, while still providing consumers the information needed to make informed choices.

Regulations often appear to be an easy way to solve problems. Want higher wages? Increase the minimum wage. Want a lower unemployment rate? Pass laws making dismissal of workers more difficult. Want higher earnings in an occupation? Restrict the entry of price-cutters. But there is a problem here: these simplistic policies do not enhance production and they ignore the secondary effects. Our living standard is directly linked to the production of goods and services that people value. Mutually advantageous trade and competitive markets encourage efficient use of resources and discovery of better ways of doing things. They help us get more value from our resources. Thus, regulatory policies that impose roadblocks against trade and entry into markets will almost always be counterproductive. If a country is going to grow and prosper, it should minimize regulations that restrict trade and the competitiveness of markets.

4. *An efficient capital market: To realize its potential, a nation must have a mechanism that channels capital into wealth-creating projects.*

While consumption is the goal of all production, it will often be necessary first to use resources to build machines, heavy equipment, and buildings, which can then be used to produce the desired consumer goods. In other words, investment increases future consumption, but it requires forgoing some present consumption. **Capital investment**—the construction and development of long-lasting resources designed to help produce more in the future—is an important potential source of economic growth. For example, the purchase of an oven by a local pizzeria will help enlarge its future output.

Resources (such as labor, land, and entrepreneurship) used to produce these **investment goods** will be unavailable for the production of consumer goods. If we consume all that we produce, no resources will be available for investment. Therefore, investment requires **saving**—a reduction in current consumption in order to make the funds available for other uses. Someone, either the investor or someone willing to supply funds to the investor, must save in order to finance investment. Saving is an integral part of the investment process.

Not all investment projects, however, are productive. An investment project will enhance the wealth of a nation only if the value of the additional output from the investment exceeds the cost. When it does not, the project is counterproductive and reduces wealth. Investments can never be made with perfect foresight, so even the most promising investment projects will sometimes fail to enhance wealth. To make the most of its potential for economic progress, a nation must have a mechanism that will attract savings and channel them into the investments that are most likely to create wealth.

In a market economy, the **capital market** performs this function.

The capital market, when defined broadly, includes the markets for stocks, bonds, and real estate. Financial institutions such as stock exchanges, banks, insurance companies, mutual funds, and investment firms play important roles in the operation of the capital market.

Private investors, such as small business owners, corporate stockholders, and **venture capitalists** place their own funds at risk in the capital market. Investors will sometimes make mistakes; sometimes they will undertake projects that prove to be unprofitable. If investors were unwilling to take such chances, many new ideas would go untested and many worthwhile but risky projects would not be undertaken.

Consider the role of entrepreneurship, risk-taking, and the capital market in the development of Internet services. In the mid-1990s, Sergey Brin and Larry Page were graduate students at Stanford University working on a research project designed to make it easier to find things on the Internet. They might have seemed unlikely candidates for entrepreneurial success. But in 1998, Brin and Page founded Google Inc., a business providing free Internet services that generates revenues through advertising. The powerful Internet search engine that they developed increases the productivity of millions of individuals and businesses each day. They have earned a fortune and Google is a household name with more than 33,000 employees in 2015. Other Internet-based companies, such as eBay and Amazon, have also earned profits and achieved growth and success during the past decade.

But the experience of numerous others was quite different. Many "dot-coms," like Broadband Sports and eVineyard, went bust because their revenues were insufficient to cover their costs. The high hopes of these firms did not materialize.

In a world of uncertainty, mistaken investments are a necessary price that must be paid for fruitful innovations in new technologies and products. Such counterproductive projects, however, must be recognized and brought to a halt. In a market economy, the capital market performs this function. If a firm continues to experience losses, eventually investors will terminate the project and stop wasting their money.

Given the pace of change and the diversity of entrepreneurial talent, the knowledge required for sound decision-making about the allocation of capital is far beyond the scope of any single leader, industrial planning committee, or government agency. Without a private capital market, there is no mechanism that can be counted on to consistently channel investment funds into wealth-creating projects.

Why? When investment funds are allocated by the government, rather than by the market, an entirely different set of factors comes into play. Political influence rather than market returns will determine which projects will be undertaken. Investment projects that reduce rather than create wealth will become far more likely.

The experiences of the centrally planned socialist economies during the Soviet era illustrate this point. For four decades (1950–1990), the investment rates in these countries were among the highest in the world. Central planners allocated approximately one-third of the national output into capital investment. Even these high rates of investment, however, did little to improve living standards because political rather than economic considerations determined which projects would be funded. Resources were often wasted on politically impractical projects and high visibility ("prestige") investments favored by important political leaders. Misdirection of investment and failure to keep up with dynamic change eventually led to the demise of socialism in most of these countries.

Recent U.S. experience with government allocation of credit for housing finance also provides insight into how political allocation of capital works. The Federal National Mortgage Association and Federal Home Loan Mortgage Corporation, commonly known as Fannie Mae and Freddie Mac, were chartered by Congress as government-sponsored corporations in 1968 and 1970, respectively. It was thought that they would improve the operation of the capital market and make home financing more affordable. Even though Fannie Mae and Freddie Mac were privately owned businesses, investors perceived that the bonds they issued to raise their funds were less risky because they were backed by the government. As a result, Fannie Mae and Freddie Mac were able to borrow funds at approximately half of a percentage point cheaper than private firms. This gave them a huge advantage over their rivals and they were highly profitable for many years.

But the government sponsorship also made Fannie Mae and Freddie Mac highly political. The president appointed several members to their boards of directors. Top management of Fannie Mae and Freddie Mac provided key congressional leaders with large political contributions and often hired away congressional staffers into high paying jobs lobbying their former bosses. Their lobbying activities were legendary. Between 1998 and 2008, Fannie Mae spent $79.5 million and Freddie Mac spent $94.9 million lobbying Congress for special favors and continuation of their privileged status.[13]

Fannie Mae and Freddie Mac did not originate mortgages; that is, they did not directly lend money to people buying houses. Instead, they purchased the mortgages in the secondary market, a market where mortgages originated by banks and other lenders are purchased. Because they had cheaper access to funds, they could purchase lots of mortgages and by the mid-1990s, these two government-sponsored enterprises held approximately 40 percent of all home mortgages. Their dominance of the secondary market was even greater. During the decade prior to their insolvency in 2008, Fannie Mae and Freddie Mac purchased more than 80 percent of the mortgages sold by banks and other mortgage originators.

---

13. These figures are from the Center for Responsive Politics, "Lobbying: Top Spenders," (2008) available at: www.opensecrets.org/lobby/top.php?indexType=s. (For additional details, see Peter J. Wallison and Charles W. Calomiris, "The Destruction of Fannie Mae and Freddie Mac," *American Enterprise Institute* (2008) available at www.aei.org /outlook/28704.

While Fannie Mae and Freddie Mac lobbied for and received favors from Congress, members of Congress used them to achieve political objectives, including making mortgage funds for housing purchases more readily available to low- and middle-income borrowers. Responding to earlier congressional directives, the Department of Housing and Urban Development mandated that, by 1996, 40 percent of the mortgages financed by Fannie Mae and Freddie Mac must go to households with incomes below the median. This figure was increased to 50 percent by 2000 and to 56 percent by 2008. In order to meet these mandates, Fannie Mae and Freddie Mac began accepting more mortgages with little or no down payment. They also substantially increased the share of mortgages granted to borrowers with a poor credit history, known as subprime borrowers. Because of their dominance of the secondary market, their lending practices exerted a huge impact on the lending standards accepted by mortgage originators. Recognizing that riskier loans could be passed on to Fannie Mae and Freddie Mac, the originators had less incentive to scrutinize the credit worthiness of borrowers or worry much about their ability to repay the funds. After all, sale of the mortgage to Fannie Mae and Freddie Mac would transfer the risk to them as well.

As Exhibit 5 shows, subprime mortgages (including those extended with incomplete documentation) soared from 4.5 percent of the new mortgages in 1994 to 13.2 percent in 2000 and to 33.6 percent of the total share of mortgage originations by 2006. During the same time frame, conventional loans, for which borrowers are required to make at least a 20 percent down payment, fell from two-thirds of the total to only one-third. The default and **foreclosure rates** for **subprime loans** range from seven to ten times the parallel rates for conventional loans to prime borrowers. Predictably, the growing share of loans to those with weaker credit eventually led to higher default and foreclosure rates.

Both Congress and the presidential administrations of Bill Clinton and George W. Bush were highly supportive of these regulatory policies

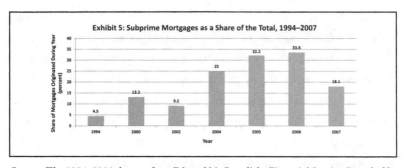

Source: The 1994–2000 data are from Edward M. Gramlich, *Financial Services Roundtable Annual Housing Policy Meeting,* Chicago, Illinois, May 21, 2004. The 2002–2007 data are from the Joint Center for Housing Studies of Harvard University, *The State of the Nation's Housing 2008,* www.jchs.harvard.edu/son/index.htm. Loans with incomplete documentation and verification, known as Alt-A loans, are included in the subprime category. Studies indicate that most of the Alt-A loans were to subprime borrowers.

and took credit for the initial increase in home ownership they helped to generate. As the policies eroded mortgage-lending standards, making credit more readily available for risky loans, the initial effects seemed positive. The demand for housing increased, housing prices soared during 2001–2005, and there was a boom in the construction industry.

But the artificially created housing boom was not sustainable. By 2004–2005, approximately half of all mortgages were either subprime (including those with incomplete documentation) or loans against the equity people had in their homes. As soon as prices leveled off and then began their decline during the second half of 2006, the house of cards came crashing down. The **mortgage default** and foreclosure rates immediately began to rise. All of this occurred well before the **recession,** which did not start until December 2007. Of course, the collapse of the housing industry eventually spread to the rest of the economy, and the bad mortgages generated huge financial problems in banking and finance both in the United States and abroad. By summer 2008, Fannie Mae and Freddie Mac were insolvent. Their operations were taken over by the government and the American taxpayer was left with approximately $400 billion of bad debt.

The interest rate policies of the Federal Reserve System also contributed to the Great Recession of 2008–2009, as we will explain in the following element. But one thing is clear: The political allocation of credit and accompanying regulatory erosion of lending standards channeled a lot of financial capital into projects that should never have been undertaken. Many homebuyers were incentivized to purchase more housing than they could afford, and that was a major contributing factor in the housing boom and subsequent bust and the recession it helped generate.

When governments are heavily involved, allocation of investment is inevitably characterized by favoritism, conflict of interest, inappropriate financial relations, and various forms of corruption. When actions of this type occur in other countries, they are often referred to as **crony capitalism.** Historically, the government has played a larger role in the allocation of investment in other countries than in the United States, but the American experience with government allocation of investment funds for housing illustrates that crony capitalism occurs in the United States as well. Regardless of the label, political allocation of capital imposes a heavy cost on citizens.

5. *Monetary stability: A stable monetary policy is*
   essential for the control of inflation, efficient
   allocation of investment, and achievement of
   economic stability.

Money is vitally important for the operation of an economy. Most importantly, money is a means of exchange. It reduces transaction costs because it provides a common denominator into which the value of all goods and services can be converted. Money also makes it possible for people to gain from complex exchanges with a time dimension, such as the sale or purchase of a home or car, which involve the receipt of income or payment of a purchase price across lengthy time periods. And it provides a means to store purchasing power for future use. Money is also a unit of account that enhances people's ability to keep track of benefits and costs, including those incurred across time periods.

The productive contribution of money, however, is directly related to the stability of its value. In this respect, money is to an economy what language is to communication. Without words that have a clearly defined meaning to both speaker and listener, communication would be difficult. So it is with money. If money does not have a stable and predictable value, it will be difficult for borrowers and lenders to find mutually agreeable terms for a loan, saving and investing will involve additional risks, and time-dimension transactions (such as payment for a house or automobile) will be fraught with additional uncertainty. When the value of money is unstable, many potentially beneficial exchanges are not made and the gains from specialization, large-scale production, and social cooperation are reduced.

There is no mystery about the cause of monetary instability. Like other commodities, the value of money is determined by supply and demand. When the supply of money is constant or increases at a slow, steady rate, the purchasing power of money will be relatively stable. In contrast, when the supply of money expands rapidly compared to the supply of goods and services, the value of money declines and prices rise. This is **inflation**. It occurs when governments print money or borrow from a central bank in order to pay their bills.[14]

Persistent inflation has a single source: rapid growth in the supply of money. The **money supply** is the total of the nation's currency, checking deposits, and traveler's checks held by individuals and businesses.

14. Supplementary readings "Consumer Price Index and Measurement of Inflation" and "Monetary Policy: How Is It Conducted and How Does It Affect the Economy?" are related to the focus of this element. These units provide additional details on inflation and money. Both units are available on the CSE website: CommonSenseEconomics.com/wp-content/uploads/CSE_Consumer-Price-Index_Inflation_Student.pdf and CommonSenseEconomics.com/wp-content/uploads/CSE_Monetary-Policy_Student.pdf.

Exhibit 6: Monetary Growth and Inflation, 1990–2014		
	Average Annual Growth Rate of Money Supply (%)	Average Annual Rate of Inflation (%)
Slow Growth of the Money Supply		
Sweden	3.0	2.3
United States	3.0	2.1
Switzerland	3.4	1.1
Singapore	3.5	1.4
United Kingdom	5.5	2.7
Central African Republic	6.4	3.6
Canada	7.5	2.1
Rapid Growth of the Money Supply		
Nigeria	22.6	23.2
Uruguay	23.0	23.4
Malawi	26.7	23.4
Ghana	29.0	24.5
Venezuela, RB	37.6	34.0
Russian Federation	41.4	39.3
Romania	46.1	53.1
Turkey	48.4	41.7
Hypergrowth of the Money Supply		
Ukraine	140.4	276.8
Zimbabwe	164.8	165.3

Source: The World Bank (WB), *World Development Indicators* (*WDI*), 2015 and International Monetary Fund, *International Financial Statistics* (annual).

Note: The data for Ghana and Venezuela are for 1990–2013. The data for Russia are for 1994–2014. The data for Ukraine are for 1993–2014. In the case of missing data, they were updated from country sources: Canada figures for 1990–2008 come from World Bank and figures for 2009–2014 come from the Canada Central Bank. The data for Zimbabwe are for 1990–2007 and come from the World Bank, *World Development Indicators 2009* report.

When that supply increases faster than the growth of the economy, the prices of goods and services will rise.

Exhibit 6 illustrates the linkage between growth of the money supply and inflation. Note how countries that increased their money supply at a slow annual rate (7.5 percent or less) experienced low rates of inflation during 1990–2014. This was true for large high-income countries like the United States and Canada, as well as for smaller ones like Sweden, Singapore, and the Central African Republic.

When the growth rate of the money supply in a country expanded more rapidly, however, the inflation rate accelerated. During 1990–2014, the money supply grew at an annual rate between 20 percent and 50 percent in Nigeria, Uruguay, Malawi, Ghana, Venezuela, Russian Federation, Romania, and Turkey. Note how these countries experienced annual inflation rates similar to their rates of monetary growth.

Extremely high rates of monetary growth (100 percent and above) lead to hyperinflation, as in Ukraine and Zimbabwe. As the growth rate of the money supply in these countries soared, so too did their rate of inflation.

As Exhibit 6 illustrates, there is a close relationship between rapid monetary expansion and high rates of inflation when measured over lengthy time periods. Historically, this linkage has been one of the most consistent relationships in all of economics.

Countries with high rates of inflation nearly always have wide fluctuations in the inflation rate. High and variable rates of inflation undermine prosperity. When prices increase 20 percent one year, 50 percent the next year, 15 percent the year after that, and so on, individuals and businesses are unable to develop sensible long-term plans. The uncertainty makes the planning and implementation of capital investment projects risky and less attractive. Unexpected changes in the inflation rate can quickly turn an otherwise profitable project into an economic disaster. Rather than dealing with these uncertainties, many decision-makers will simply forgo capital investments and other transactions involving long-term commitments. Some will even move their business and investment activities to countries with a more stable environment. As a result, potential gains from trade, business activities, and capital formation will be lost.

Moreover, when governments pursue inflationary policies, people will spend less time producing and more time trying to protect their wealth. Because failure to accurately anticipate the rate of inflation can devastate one's wealth, individuals will shift scarce resources away from the production of goods and services and toward actions designed to hedge against inflation. The ability of business decision-makers to forecast changes in prices becomes more valuable than their ability to manage and organize production. When the inflation rate is uncertain, businesses will shy away from entering into long-term contracts, place many investment projects on hold, and divert resources and time into less productive activities. Funds will flow into the purchase of gold, silver, and art objects, in the hope that their prices will rise with inflation, rather than into more productive investments such as buildings, machines, and technological research. As resources move from more productive to less productive activities, economic progress slows.

Economic progress will also be undermined when monetary policymakers are constantly shifting between monetary expansion and contraction. When the monetary authorities expand the money supply rapidly, initially the more expansionary **monetary policy** will generally push interest rates downward, stimulating current investment and creating an artificial economic boom. However, the boom will not be sustainable. If the expansionary monetary policy continues, it will generate inflation, which will cause monetary policy-makers to shift toward a more restrictive policy. As they do so, interest rates will rise, which will impede **private investment** and throw the economy into a recession. Thus, monetary shifts between expansion and restriction will generate economic instability, jerking the economy back and forth between booms and busts. This pattern of monetary policy will also create uncertainty, slow private investment, and reduce the rate of economic growth.

This is exactly what happened between 1968 and 1982 in the United States. The monetary authorities followed an expansionary policy that

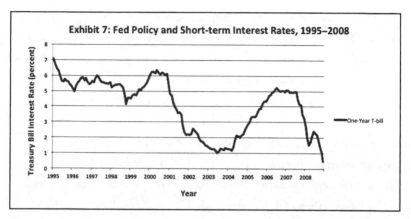

Source: Federal Reserve System.

fueled inflation and, as the inflation rate rose, the policy-makers shifted toward restriction, which threw the economy into a recession. The recessions of 1970, 1974–1975, 1980, and 1982 were primarily the result of the "speed up and slow down" monetary policy of that era.

More recently, expansionary monetary policy pushed short-term interest rates to then-historic low levels during 2002–2004, as policy-makers sought to stimulate a more rapid recovery from the recession of 2001. As Exhibit 7 shows, the one-year Treasury bill interest rate was maintained at 2 percent or less throughout 2002, 2003, and 2004. This expansionary monetary policy, coupled with the regulations that eroded lending standards discussed in the previous element, generated a housing market boom. However, as the inflation rate rose during 2005, the Fed shifted to a more restrictive monetary policy and interest rates rose. This slowed the housing price inflation, but it also soon led to soaring mortgage default and housing foreclosure rates, and eventually to the Great Recession of 2008.[15]

15. For a comprehensive analysis of monetary policy and the crisis of 2008, see John Taylor, *Getting Off Track: How Government Actions and Interventions Caused, Prolonged, and Worsened the Financial Crisis* (Stanford: Hoover Institution Press, 2009).

The combination of regulations promoting loose mortgage lending standards and the Fed's artificially low interest rate policies encouraged decision-makers to borrow more money and make housing investments beyond what they could afford. While the policy created a housing construction boom during 2002–2005, many of these investments were uneconomical. They should never have been undertaken. They comprise what economists call **mal-investment**. Before an economy can return to a sustainable path of growth, these badly allocated investments will have to be cleansed from the system. As the severe contraction which started December of 2007 and ended June 2009 illustrates, this is a costly and painful process.

Monetary stability is an essential ingredient of the environment for economic progress. Without monetary stability, potential gains from capital investment and other exchanges involving time commitments will be eroded and the people of the country will fail to realize their full potential.

6. Low tax rates: People produce more when they can keep more of what they earn.

Taxes are paid in the sweat of every man who labors. If those taxes are excessive, they are reflected in idle factories, in tax-sold farms, and in hordes of hungry people tramping streets and seeking jobs in vain.
—Franklin D. Roosevelt, Pittsburgh, October 19, 1932

When high tax rates take a large share of income, the incentive to work and use resources productively declines. The **marginal tax rate** is particularly important. This is the share of additional income that is taxed away at any given income level. For example, in the United States in 2015, if a taxpayer with $60,000 in taxable income earned an extra $100, he or she had to pay $25 of that $100 in federal income tax. Therefore, the taxpayer faced a marginal tax rate of 25 percent.

As marginal tax rates increase, the share of additional earnings that people get to keep decline. For example, at the 25 percent marginal tax rate, individuals are permitted to keep $75 if they earn an additional $100. But, if the marginal tax rate rose to 40 percent, then the taxpayer would only get to keep $60 out of a $100 increase in earnings.

There are three reasons why high marginal tax rates will reduce output and income. First, high marginal tax rates discourage work effort and reduce the productivity of labor. When marginal tax rates soar to 55 or 60 percent, individuals get to keep less than half of their additional earnings. When people are not allowed to keep much of what they earn, they tend not to earn very much. Some, perhaps people with working spouses, will drop out of the labor force. Others will simply work fewer hours, retire earlier, or take jobs with longer vacations or a more preferred location. Still others will be more particular about accepting jobs when unemployed, refuse to move to take a job or to gain a pay raise, or forget about pursuing that promising but risky business venture. High tax rates can even drive a nation's most productive citizens to countries where taxes are lower. Such movements will reduce the size and productivity of the available labor supply, causing output to decline.

Of course, most people will not immediately quit work, or even work less diligently, in response to an increase in the marginal tax rate. A person who has spent years training for a particular occupation will probably continue working—and working hard—especially if that person is in the peak earning years of life. But many younger people who have not already made costly investments in specialized training will be discouraged from doing so by high marginal tax rates. Thus some of the negative effects of high tax rates on work effort will be felt in the form of reduced productivity for many years in the future.

High tax rates will also cause some people to shift to activities in which they are less productive because they do not have to pay taxes on them. For example, high taxes will drive up the costs of skilled painters, perhaps leading you to paint your own house, even though you lack the skill to do it efficiently. Without high tax rates, the professional painter would do the job at a cost you could afford, and you could spend your time doing work for which you are better suited. Waste and economic inefficiency result from these tax-distorted incentives.

Second, high marginal tax rates will reduce both the level and efficiency of capital formation. High tax rates repel foreign investment and cause domestic investors to search for investment projects abroad where both taxes and production costs are lower than at home. This reduces investment and the availability of productive equipment, which provides the fuel for economic growth. Domestic investors will also turn to projects that shelter current income from taxation, and away from projects with a higher rate of return but fewer tax-avoidance benefits. These tax shelters enable people to gain personally from projects that do not enhance the value of resources. Again, scarce capital is wasted, and resources are channeled away from their most productive uses.

Third, high marginal tax rates encourage individuals to consume tax-deductible goods in place of nondeductible goods, even though the nondeductible goods may be more desirable. When purchases are tax deductible, individuals who purchase them do not bear their full cost, because the expenditure reduces the taxes they would otherwise pay. When marginal tax rates are high, tax-deductible expenditures become relatively cheap.

The sales of the British-made luxury car Rolls-Royce in the 1970s provides a vivid illustration of this point. During this era, the marginal income tax rates in the United Kingdom were as high as 98 percent on large incomes. A business owner paying that tax rate could buy a car as a tax-deductible business expense, so why not buy an exotic, more expensive car? The purchase would reduce the owner's profit by the car's price—say £100,000—but the owner would have received only £2,000 of his or her profit anyway, because the 98 percent marginal tax rate would have reduced the £100,000 to £2,000. In effect, the government was paying 98 percent of the car's costs (through lost tax revenue). When the UK cut the top marginal tax rate to 70 percent, the sales of Rolls-Royces plummeted. After the rate reduction, the £100,000 car now cost the business owner not £2,000 but £30,000. The lower marginal rates made it much more expensive for wealthy Brits to purchase Rolls-Royces, and they responded by reducing their purchases.

High marginal rates artificially reduce the personal cost, but not the cost to society, of items that are tax deductible or that can be taken as a business expense. Predictably, taxpayers confronting high marginal tax rates will spend more money on such tax-deductible items as plush offices, Hawaiian business conferences, business entertainment, and a company-provided automobile. Because such tax-deductible expenditures reduce their taxes, people will often buy goods they would not buy if they were paying the full cost. Waste and inefficiency are byproducts of high marginal tax rates and the perverse incentives they generate.

Reductions in tax rates, particularly high rates, can increase the incentive to earn and improve the efficiency of resource use. The United States has had three major reductions in tax rates: the rate reductions during the 1920s in the aftermath of World War I, the Kennedy tax cuts of the 1960s, and the Reagan tax cuts of the 1980s. All were followed by strong and lengthy expansions in real output.

In contrast, large tax increases can exert a disastrous impact on the economy. The tax policy during the Great Depression illustrates this point. Seeking to reduce the federal budget deficit in 1932, the Republican Hoover administration and the Democratic Congress passed the largest peacetime tax rate increase in the history of the United States.

The lowest marginal tax rate on personal income was raised from 1.5 percent to 4 percent. At the top of the income scale, the highest marginal tax rate was raised from 25 percent to 63 percent. Essentially, personal income tax rates were more than doubled in one year! This huge tax increase reduced the after-tax income of households and the incentive to earn, consume, save, and invest. The results were catastrophic. In 1932, real output fell by 13 percent, the largest single-year decline during the Great Depression era. Unemployment rose from 15.9 percent in 1931 to 23.6 percent in 1932.

Just four years later, the Roosevelt administration increased taxes again, pushing the top marginal rate to 79 percent in 1936. Thus, during the latter half of the 1930s, high earners were permitted to keep only 21 cents of each additional dollar they earned. (Note: It is interesting to contrast the words of candidate Roosevelt presented at the top of this element with the tax policy followed during his presidency.) Several other factors, including a huge contraction in the money supply and a large increase in tariff rates, contributed to both the severity and length of the Great Depression. But it is also clear that the tax increases of both the Hoover and Roosevelt administrations played a major role in this tragic chapter of American history.[16]

The disincentive effects of high marginal tax rates are not just an issue for those with high earnings. Many people with relatively low incomes also confront high implicit marginal tax rates, the combination of additional taxes plus the loss of benefits from income-tested transfer programs. For example, suppose that an individual's income increases from $20,000 to $30,000 and, as a result, income and payroll taxes take 30 percent of the additional earnings. Further, because of this increase in income, the

16. For additional information on taxes and other dimensions of economic policy during the Great Depression era, see supplementary reading "Lessons from the Great Depression," available on the CSE website: CommonSenseEconomics.com/wp-content/uploads/GreatDepressionAnnouncement.pdf.

individual loses $5,000 in benefits from food stamps, Medicaid, and other transfer programs. He or she would confront an implicit marginal tax rate of 80 percent! Thirty percent would come in the form of a higher tax bill and an additional 50 percent in the form of lost transfer benefits.

People in this position who earn an additional $10,000 get to keep only 20 percent of it. Obviously, this will substantially reduce their incentive to earn and make it more difficult to move up the income ladder. We will return to this issue in Part 3, Element 8, when examining the impact of transfer programs on the poverty rate.

In summary, economic analysis indicates that high tax rates, including implicit rates reflecting the loss of transfer benefits, will reduce productive activity, impede both employment and investment, and promote wasteful use of resources. They are an obstacle to prosperity and the growth of income. Moreover, large tax rate increases during a period of economic weakness can exert a disastrous impact on the economy.

7. *Free trade: People achieve higher incomes when they are free to trade with people in other countries.*

> *Free trade consists simply in letting people buy and sell as they want to buy and sell. Protective tariffs are as much applications of force as are blockading squadrons, and their objective is the same—to prevent trade. The difference between the two is that blockading squadrons are a means whereby nations seek to prevent their enemies from trading; protective tariffs are a means whereby nations attempt to prevent their own people from trading.*[17]
>
> —HENRY GEORGE, NINETEENTH-CENTURY
> POLITICAL ECONOMIST

17. Henry George, *Protection or Free Trade* (New York: Robert Schalkenbach Foundation, 1980).

The principles involved in international trade are basically the same as those underlying any voluntary exchange. As is the case with domestic trade, international trade makes it possible for each of the trading partners to produce and consume more goods and services than would otherwise be possible. There are three reasons why this is so.

First, the people of each nation benefit if they can acquire a product or service through trade more cheaply than they can produce it domestically. Resource endowments differ substantially across countries. Goods that are costly to produce in one country may be economical to produce in another. For example, countries with warm, moist climates such as Brazil and Colombia find it advantageous to specialize in the production of coffee. People in Canada and Australia, where land is abundant and population sparse, tend to specialize in land-intensive products, such as wheat, feed grains, and beef. The citizens of Japan, where land is scarce and the labor force highly skilled, specialize in manufacturing such items as cameras, automobiles, and electronic products. Trade will permit each of the trading partners to use more of their resources to produce and sell things they do well rather than having them tied up producing things at a high cost. As a result of this specialization and trade, total output increases and people in each country are able to achieve a higher standard of living than would otherwise be attainable.

Second, international trade allows domestic producers and consumers to benefit from the economies of scale typical of many large operations. This point is particularly important for small countries. With international trade, domestic producers can operate on a larger scale and therefore achieve lower per-unit costs than would be possible if they were solely dependent on their domestic market. For example, trade makes it possible for textile manufacturers in countries like Costa Rica, Guatemala, Thailand, and Vietnam to enjoy the benefits of large-scale production. If they were unable to sell abroad, their costs per unit would be much higher because their domestic textile markets are too small to support large, low-cost firms in this industry. With international trade, however, textile firms in these countries can produce and sell large quantities and compete effectively in the world market.

International trade also allows domestic consumers to benefit by purchasing from large-scale producers abroad. Given the huge design and engineering costs of airplanes today, for example, no country has a domestic market large enough to permit even a single airplane manufacturer to realize fully the economies of large-scale production. With international trade, however, Boeing and Airbus can sell many more planes, each at a lower cost. As a result, consumers in every nation can fly in planes purchased economically from such large-scale producers.

Third, international trade promotes competition in domestic markets and allows consumers to purchase a wider variety of goods at lower prices. Competition from abroad keeps domestic producers on their toes. It forces them to improve the quality of their products and keep costs down. At the same time, the variety of goods available from abroad provides consumers with a much greater array of choices than would be available without international trade.

Governments often impose regulations that restrain international trade. These can be tariffs (taxes on imported goods), quotas (limits on the amount imported), **exchange rate** controls (artificially holding down the value of the domestic currency to discourage imports and encourage exports), or bureaucratic regulations on importers or exporters. All such trade restrictions increase transaction costs and reduce the gains from exchange. As Henry George noted in the quote in the beginning of this element, trade restraints are like a military blockade that a nation imposes on its own people. Just as a blockade imposed by an enemy will harm a nation, imposing a blockade in the form of trade restrictions also harms the nation.

Is the United States a free trade country? Many Americans think it is, but that is not entirely true. The United States imposes tariffs of

10 percent or higher on more than 1,000 product categories, including footwear and apparel. The United States also imposes quotas on dairy products, sugar, ethanol, cotton, beef, canned tuna, and tobacco. Imports above the quotas are subject to prohibitively high tariffs. In addition, procedures imposed in the aftermath of September 11, 2001, have made it both costlier and time-consuming to clear goods through U.S. customs.

Noneconomists often argue that import restrictions can create jobs. As we discussed in Part 1, Element 9, it is production of value that really matters, not jobs. If jobs were the key to high incomes, we could easily create as many as we wanted. All of us could work one day digging holes and the next day filling them up. We would all be employed, but we would also be exceedingly poor because such jobs would not generate goods and services that people value.

Import restrictions may appear to expand employment because the industries shielded by restraints may increase in size or at least remain steady. This does not mean, however, that the restrictions expand total employment. Remember the secondary effects discussed in Part 1, Element 12. When Americans erect tariffs, quotas, and other barriers limiting the ability of foreigners to sell in the United States, they are simultaneously reducing foreigners' ability to buy from Americans. Our imports provide people in other countries with the purchasing power they need to buy our exports. If foreigners sell less to Americans, they will have fewer of the dollars required to buy from Americans. Thus import restrictions will indirectly reduce exports. Output and employment in export industries will decline, offsetting any jobs "saved" in the protected industries.[18]

18. Many of the "job savers" act as if foreigners are willing to supply us with goods without ever using their acquired dollars to purchase things from us. But this is not the case. If foreigners were willing to sell things to us for dollars and never use the dollars to buy products from us, it would be as though we could write checks for anything we wanted without anyone ever cashing them. Wouldn't that be great? In fact, however, people do cash our checks when we buy things from them. They don't actually want our checks; they want the money

Trade restrictions neither create nor destroy jobs; they reshuffle them.[19] The restrictions artificially direct workers and other resources toward the production of things that we produce at a higher cost than others do. Output and employment shrink in areas where our resources are more productive—areas where our firms could compete successfully in the world market if it were not for the impact of the restrictions. Thus labor and other resources are shifted away from areas where their productivity is high and moved into areas where it is low. Such policies reduce both the output and income levels of Americans.

Many Americans believe that U.S. workers cannot compete with foreigners who sometimes make as little as $2 or $3 per day. This view is wrong and stems from a misunderstanding of both the source of high wages and the law of comparative advantage. Workers in the United States are well-educated, possess a high skill level, and work with large amounts of capital equipment. These factors contribute to their high productivity, which is the source of their high wages. In low-wage countries like Mexico and China, wages are low precisely because productivity is low.

Each country will always have some things that it does relatively better than others. Both high- and low-wage countries will benefit when

---

represented by the checks so they can buy things from us. Similarly, people in other countries who export products to us don't want our money; they want what the money can buy. Otherwise, we could just print the dollars we send them to get their goods as cheaply as possible, without fear of inflation, because the dollars would not come back to buy things in our market. But most of the dollars do come back in the form of foreign purchases. Thus, our purchases from foreigners—our imports—generate the demand for our exports.

19. When the exchange rate is determined by market forces, equilibrium in this market will bring the purchases of goods, services, and assets (including both real and financial assets such as bonds) from foreigners into balance with the sale of these items to foreigners. During the last couple of decades, United States imports of goods and services have persistently exceeded exports. With market-determined exchange rates, such trade deficits will be largely offset by an inflow of capital of similar magnitude. The capital inflow will result in lower interest rates, more investment, and additional employment. Thus, even in this case, there is no reason to anticipate that there will be a negative impact on employment. The U.S. experience illustrates this point. Even though trade deficits were present throughout most of the 1980–2005 period, employment in the United States expanded by more than 35 million.

they can focus on using more of their resources pursuing productive activities that they do comparatively well. If a high-wage country can import a product from foreign producers at a lower cost than it can be produced domestically, importing it makes sense. Fewer of our resources will be tied up producing items that could be supplied domestically only at a high cost, and more will be directed toward production of things that we do well—goods and services that domestic producers can supply at a low cost.[20] Trade will make it possible for workers in both high- and low-wage countries to produce a larger output than would otherwise be possible. In turn, the higher level of productivity will lead to higher wages for both.

What if foreign producers were able to provide consumers with a good so cheap that domestic producers were unable to compete? The sensible thing to do would be to accept the economical goods and use domestic resources to produce other things. Remember, it is availability of goods and services, not jobs, that determines our living standards. The French economist Frédéric Bastiat dramatically highlighted this point in his 1845 satire, "A Petition on Behalf of the Candlestick Makers." The petition was supposedly written to the French Chamber of Deputies by French producers of candles, lanterns, and other products providing indoor lighting. The petition complained that domestic suppliers of lighting were "suffering from the ruinous competition of a foreign rival who apparently works under conditions so superior to our own for production of light that he is flooding the domestic market with it at an incredibly low price; for the moment he appears, our sales cease, all the consumers turn to him, and a branch of the French industry whose ramifications are innumerable is all at once reduced to complete stagnation."

20. The same logic applies to "outsourcing," undertaking certain activities abroad in order to reduce cost. If an activity can be handled at a lower cost abroad, doing so will release domestic resources that can be employed in higher productive activities. As a result, output will be larger and income levels higher.

Of course this rival is the sun, and the petitioners are requesting that the Deputies pass a law requiring the closing of windows, blinds, and other openings so that sunlight cannot enter buildings. The petition goes on to list the occupations in the lighting industry in which there would be a large increase in employment if the use of the sun for indoor lighting was outlawed. Bastiat's point in this satire is clear: As silly as the proposed legislation in the petition is, it is no sillier than legislation that reduces the availability of low-cost goods and services in order to "save" domestic producers and promote employment.[21]

During the past three decades, transportation costs have fallen and trade barriers have declined. The reduction in trade barriers has been most pronounced in low-income countries. In 1980, it was commonplace for poor, **less-developed countries** to impose tariffs of 20 percent or more. Many also imposed exchange rate controls, which made it difficult for their citizens to get their hands on the foreign currency needed to purchase imports. Today, the situation is dramatically different. Beginning in the 1980s, numerous less-developed countries including China and India lowered their tariffs, relaxed exchange rate controls, and removed other trade barriers. As a result, international trade has grown rapidly.

The growth of international trade has made it possible for the world to produce a larger output and achieve a higher level of consumption than otherwise would have been the case. Per capita income has increased rapidly in many less-developed countries, particularly the populous nations of Asia. The poor in particular have benefited from the freer trade, and worldwide, nearly a billion people moved out of extreme poverty in the twenty years from 1990 to 2010.[22]

---

21. An abridged version of Frédéric Bastiat's "Competition with the Sun" is available on the CSE website: CommonSenseEconomics.com/wp-content/uploads/Bastiat_Unfair CompetitionSun.pdf.
22. See "The World's Next Great Leap Forward Towards the End of Poverty." *Economist* (June 2013): n.p. www.economist.com/news/leaders/21578665-nearly-1-billion-people -have-been-taken-out-extreme-poverty-20-years-world-should-aim.

Further, the growth of international trade has narrowed the income gap between rich and poor nations. In recent decades, less-developed countries have grown more rapidly than high-income developed nations. Moreover, the growth of income has been particularly rapid in China and India, home to nearly one-third of the world's population. As a result, the distribution of income worldwide is now more equal than it was in 1980.[23]

However, the impact of the expansion in trade on the distribution of income is often different in high-income countries such as the United States, Canada, Japan, and those of Western Europe. Predictably, high-income countries will tend to export goods requiring lots of high-skill, well-educated labor while disproportionately importing goods produced by low-skill labor. Thus, trade may increase the demand for high-skill labor relative to low-skill labor. To the extent that this is the case, the earnings of high-skill workers will rise relative to low-skill workers, increasing domestic income inequality. Income inequality has increased in almost all high-income countries in recent decades, and the growth of international trade may well be a contributing factor.

Currently, there appears to be a surge in hostility toward international trade in several high-income countries, including the United States. Leading political figures have called for various types of trade barriers, particularly restrictions directed toward imports from poor countries. The increased income inequality and slow growth in the earnings of low-skill, poorly educated workers contributes to this hostility. But there is another crucially important factor here: the political power of well-organized interests. Trade restrictions benefit specific producers and their resource suppliers, including some workers, at the expense of consumers and suppliers in other industries. Typically, industries

---

23. For evidence that income inequality worldwide has declined since 1980, see Xavier Sala-i-Martin, "The World Distribution of Income: Falling Poverty and . . . Convergence, Period," *The Quarterly Journal of Economics* 121, No. 2 (2006): 351–97.

lobbying the government for protection against foreign rivals are well-organized and their gains are concentrated and highly visible, while consumers, other workers, and other resource suppliers are generally poorly organized and their gains from international trade widely dispersed. Predictably, the organized interests will have more political clout (contributions and other forms of political support), providing politicians with a strong incentive to cater to their views.

Furthermore, it is easy to see the harm to the workers who lose their jobs when steel, for example, is produced more cheaply abroad and freely imported. In contrast, the gains of those helped by the freer trade are much less visible. In the case of trade restrictions, sound economic thinking often conflicts with a winning political strategy.

History indicates that the growing hostility to trade is potentially dangerous. As the economy slowed in the late 1920s, a similar hostility toward trade developed. This led to the passage of the Smoot-Hawley trade bill at mid-year 1930. This legislation increased tariffs by more than 50 percent on approximately 3,200 imported products. President Herbert Hoover, Senator Reed Smoot, Congressman Willis Hawley, and other proponents of the bill thought higher tariffs would stimulate the economy and save jobs. As Hawley put it, "I want to see American workers employed producing American goods for American consumption."[24]

While the rhetoric sounded great, the results were dramatically different. The tariff increase angered foreigners, and sixty countries responded with higher tariffs on American products. International trade plunged and so did output in the United States. By 1932 the volume of U.S. trade had fallen to less than half the level prior to the bill. Gains from trade were lost, the tariff revenues of the federal government actually fell, output and employment plunged, and the unemployment rate

---

24. As quoted in Frank Whitson Fetter, "Congressional Tariff Theory," *American Economic Review* 23 (September 1933): 413–27.

soared. Unemployment stood at 7.8 percent when the Smoot-Hawley bill was passed, but it ballooned to 23.6 percent just two years later. The stock market, which had regained almost all of the October 1929 losses prior to passage of Smoot-Hawley, plunged during the months following adoption.

More than a thousand economists signed an open letter to President Hoover warning of the harmful effects of Smoot-Hawley and pleading with him not to sign the legislation. He rejected their pleas, but history confirmed the validity of their warnings. Other factors, such as the sharp contraction in the money supply and the huge tax increases of both 1932 and 1936 contributed to the Great Depression. But the Smoot-Hawley trade bill was also a major cause of the tragic events of that era.[25]

Will history repeat itself? Hopefully not, but the experience of the 1930s indicates that uninformed political rhetoric and hostility toward trade can lead to catastrophic results.

The Importance of Institutions and Policies: Concluding Thoughts

During the past two decades, there has been a virtual explosion of scholarly research providing support for the view that **economic institutions** and policies are the primary determinant of economic growth and development. By economic institutions, we mean the legal requirements, regulations, traditions, and customs that create the framework in which an economy operates. They include constitutional mandates, legal processes, rules that govern exchange, and the structure of monetary arrangements.

---

25. For additional information on the impact of the Smoot-Hawley legislation and other dimensions of economic policy during the Great Depression era, see supplementary reading "Lessons from the Great Depression," available on the CSE website: Common SenseEconomics.com/wp-content/uploads/GreatDepressionAnnouncement.pdf.

(Policies are more specific political actions that can be altered more quickly than institutions.)

The area of study that analyzes the impact of institutions and policies on economic growth, development, and performance is known as the New Institutional Economics. According to this view, institutions and policies that encourage productive actions and discourage predatory behavior provide the key to growth and prosperity. While there is some debate about the precise institutions that are most appropriate for the achievement of rapid growth, there is considerable agreement that secure property rights, open markets, monetary stability, and minimal trade restrictions are central to the establishment of a sound institutional environment. The points outlined in this section are reflective of the new institutional view.

How much do institutions and policies matter? In order to answer this question, we need a way of comparing the institutions and policies of different countries. In the mid-1980s, the Fraser Institute of Vancouver, Canada, began work on a special project designed to develop a cross-country measure of economic freedom. Several leading scholars, including Nobel Laureates Milton Friedman, Gary Becker, and Douglass North, participated in the endeavor. This project culminated with the development of the Economic Freedom of the World (EFW) index.[26] Now published by a worldwide network of eighty institutes, this index measures the extent to which a country's institutions and policies are consistent with economic freedom—that is, with personal choice, private ownership, voluntary exchange, and competitive markets. The index incorporates forty-two separate components and provides ratings for approximately one hundred countries throughout the 1980–2013 period.

In many ways the EFW index reflects the elements outlined above. To

26. For additional details, see James Gwartney, Robert Lawson, and Joshua Hall, *Economic Freedom of the World: 2015 Annual Report* (Vancouver: Fraser Institute, 2015) and the website www.freetheworld.com.

achieve a high EFW rating, a country must provide secure protection of privately owned property, evenhanded enforcement of contracts, and a stable monetary environment. It also must keep taxes low, refrain from creating barriers to both domestic and international trade, and rely more fully on markets rather than government expenditures and regulations to allocate goods and resources. If these institutional and policy factors really do affect economic performance, countries with persistently high EFW ratings should do much better than those with persistently low ratings.

Exhibit 8 presents data on the 2013 per capita income and its growth for the ten countries with the highest and lowest EFW ratings during 1990–2013. Among the 113 countries and jurisdictions for which the EFW data were available over the twenty-three-year period, Hong Kong, Singapore, New Zealand, Switzerland, and the United States headed the list of the most persistently free economies. At the other end of the spectrum, the Democratic Republic of the Congo, Guinea-Bissau, Venezuela, Zimbabwe, and the Republic of the Congo were the least-free economies. The average per capita income of the ten most-free economies was $52,445, more than twelve times the figure ($4,164) for the ten least-free economies. Not only did the ten most-free economies have a substantially higher income level, they also grew more rapidly. The growth rate of per capita GDP of the ten most-free economies averaged 2.0 percent annually during 1990–2013, compared to negative 0.2 percent for the ten least-free economies.

Exhibits 9a and 9b break the 113 countries into quartiles arrayed from low to high by their EFW rating and then present data for the average income level and growth rate for each of the four groups. The same pattern emerges: The freer economies among the 113 countries both achieve higher per capita income levels and grow more rapidly. The most-free countries had an average 2013 per capita income of $38,601, approximately 5.5 times the average for the least-free countries. Similarly, the average annual growth rate of the top group was 3.27 percent, compared

Exhibit 8: Economic Freedom, GDP Per Capita, and Growth			
	EFW Rating, 1990–2013	GDP Per Capita 2013 PPP (constant 2011 international $)	Growth Rate of GDP Per Capita 1990–2013 PPP (percent, constant 2011 international $)
10 Highest Rated Countries			
Hong Kong	9.0	$51,656	2.9%
Singapore	8.7	$77,721	3.6%
New Zealand	8.3	$33,360	1.4%
Switzerland	8.3	$54,983	0.7%
United States	8.2	$51,282	1.4%
United Kingdom	8.2	$36,908	1.5%
Canada	8.1	$42,213	1.3%
Australia	8.0	$42,840	1.8%
Ireland	7.9	$44,640	3.0%
Luxembourg	7.8	$88,850	2.0%
Average	**8.2**	**$52,445**	**2.0%**
10 Lowest Rated Countries			
Nigeria	5.2	$3,030	2.6%
Sierra Leone	5.2	$1,334	1.5%
Central Afr. Rep.	5.0	$944	−2.1%
Burundi	5.0	$1,051	−1.5%
Algeria	4.7	$10,113	1.1%
Congo, Rep. of	4.7	$5,264	0.3%
Zimbabwe	4.7	$2,532	−1.5%
Venezuela	4.6	$14,539	0.8%
Guinea-Bissau	4.4	$1,564	−0.6%
Congo, Dem. R.	4.4	$1,270	−2.4%
Average	**4.8**	**$4,164**	**−0.2%**

Source: Derived from World Bank, *World Development Indicators,* and Gwartney, et al., *Economic Freedom of the World: 2015 Annual Report.*

Note: Libya, Syria, and Myanmar were in the original bottom ten but they are omitted here because the GDP data are unavailable.

to 1.17 percent for the bottom group. Note the strong positive relationship between economic freedom and per capita GDP across quartiles.

When low-income countries get the institutions and policies right, they are able to achieve exceedingly high growth rates and narrow the income gap relative to high-income industrial nations. Countries and jurisdictions like Hong Kong, Singapore, Taiwan, Ireland, Chile, Mauritius, and Botswana illustrate this point. During recent decades, all of

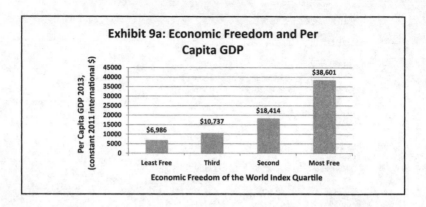

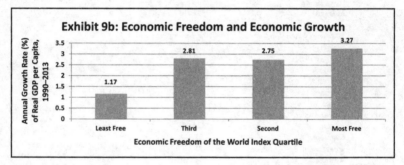

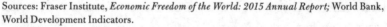

Sources: Fraser Institute, *Economic Freedom of the World: 2015 Annual Report;* World Bank, World Development Indicators.

Note: The growth data were adjusted to control for the initial level of income.

these countries have made substantial moves toward economic freedom, and all of them have grown rapidly and achieved substantial increases in income levels and living standards. In 1980 the two most populous countries, China and India, were also among the world's least free economies. During the 1980s and 1990s, they adopted policies more consistent with economic freedom, and they, too, are now achieving impressive rates of economic growth.

Since the mid-1980s, many less-developed countries have moved substantially toward economic freedom. The countries moving the most toward economic freedom have grown more rapidly. This has been a major contributing factor to the sharp decline in the world's poverty rate. The World Bank classifies a person as living in "extreme poverty" if his or her income is less than $1.25 per day. In 2005, the world's extreme poverty rate was 25 percent, down from 58 percent in 1980. Thus, the extreme poverty rate is now less than half the figure of a quarter century ago.

Persons with incomes of less than $2 per day are classified as living in moderate poverty. The world's moderate poverty rate fell from 75 percent in 1980 to 46 percent in 2005. Less-developed countries with the highest economic freedom ratings and/or the largest increases in economic freedom achieved the largest reductions in poverty during 1980–2005.[27]

Both economic theory and the empirical evidence indicate that countries grow more rapidly, achieve higher income levels, and make more progress against poverty when they adopt and maintain policies along the lines outlined in this section. The key to economic progress is to get the institutions and policies right. The sooner citizens and political leaders around the world become aware of this point and begin moving their countries toward greater economic freedom, the more prosperous the world will be.

---

27. See Joseph Connors and James Gwartney, "Economic Freedom and Global Poverty" in *Accepting the Invisible Hand,* ed. Mark D. White (New York: Palgrave Macmillan, 2010).

PART 3

*Ten Key Elements of Economic Thinking
About the Role of Government*

TEN KEY ELEMENTS OF
ECONOMIC THINKING ABOUT
THE ROLE OF GOVERNMENT

1. Government promotes economic progress by protecting the rights of individuals and supplying a few goods that are difficult to provide through markets.

2. When monopoly is present and barriers to entry high, markets will fail to achieve ideal efficiency.

3. Public goods and externalities result in incentives that may encourage self-interested individuals to undertake activities that are inconsistent with ideal economic efficiency.

4. Allocation through political voting is fundamentally different than market allocation.

5. Unless restrained by constitutional rules, special-interest groups will use the democratic political process to obtain government favors at the expense of others.

6. Unless restrained by constitutional rules, legislators will run budget deficits and spend excessively.

7. When governments become heavily involved in providing favors to some at the expense of others, inefficiency results and improper, unethical relationships develop between government officials and businesses.

8. The net gain of transfer recipients is less, and often substantially less, than the amount of the transfer.

9. The economy is far too complex to be centrally planned and efforts to do so will result in inefficiency and cronyism.

10. Competition is just as important in government as in markets.

Introduction

Economists use the standard of economic efficiency to assess the operation of an economy. When resources are used efficiently, only actions that yield more benefits than costs are undertaken. No action will be undertaken that costs more than it is worth. Put simply, **economic efficiency** means getting the most value from the available resources. Courses in economics generally explain why markets will fail to achieve ideal efficiency for certain categories of activity and highlight what the government might do to improve the situation. We follow this convention—we consider the potential of idealized political action, but we also apply the tools of economics to the operation of the political process.

Government expenditures now constitute 40 percent or more of national income in the United States and several other countries. Given its size and scope, understanding how political allocation works is vitally important. During the past half century, this topic has become an integral part of economics. Economists use the term **public choice** when referring to this area of study.[1] Part 3 will incorporate this analysis.

---

1. James Buchanan was awarded the 1986 Nobel Prize in Economics for his role in the development of public choice economics. For a clear and comprehensive presentation of

Democratic governments often use taxes and borrowing to provide some with transfers, subsidies, and other forms of favoritism. We will analyze this process and explain why the impact of these programs is different, and often substantially different, than most believe. Part 3 will also outline a set of constitutional rules that might improve the operation of government and its potential to enhance the quality of our lives. We hope you find our approach stimulating and that it will challenge you to think more seriously about both the potential and limitations of the political process.

1. *Government promotes economic progress by protecting the rights of individuals and supplying a few goods that are difficult to provide through markets.*

> *A wise and frugal government, which shall restrain men from injuring one another, which shall leave them otherwise free to regulate their own pursuits of industry and improvements, and shall not take from the mouth of labor the bread it has earned. This is the sum of good government.*[2]
>
> —THOMAS JEFFERSON

Governments play a vitally important economic role. Governments can promote social cooperation and enhance the welfare of the citizenry through the performance of two major functions: (1) the protective function that provides people with protection for their lives, liberties, and properties; and (2) the productive function that supplies a few select goods that have unusual characteristics that make them difficult to provide through markets.

---

public choice analysis, see Randy Simmons, *Beyond Politics: The Roots of Government Failure* (Oakland, California: The Independent Institute, 2011).
2. Thomas Jefferson, First Inaugural Address, March 4, 1801.

The **protective function** encompasses the government's maintenance of a framework of security and order, including the enforcement of rules against theft, fraud, and violence. Governments are granted a monopoly on the legitimate use of force in order to protect citizens from each other and from outsiders. Thus the "protective state" seeks to prevent individuals from harming one another and maintains an infrastructure of rules that allow people to interact with one another cooperatively and harmoniously. A legal system that protects individuals and their property from aggressors, enforces contracts in an unbiased manner, and provides equal treatment under the law (see Part 2, Element 1) forms the core of the protective function of government.

The protective function is crucially important for the smooth operation of markets. When the government clearly defines and enforces property rights, market prices will reflect the opportunity cost of resources, and producers will be directed toward production of the goods and services that are most highly valued by consumers compared to their cost. Moreover, if contracts are enforced in a way that is efficient and without favoritism, transaction costs will be low and the volume of trade enlarged. In turn, the incentive structure will encourage people to develop resources, engage in mutually advantageous trade, and undertake wealth-creating projects.

It is difficult to overstate the importance of the government's protective function. When this function is performed well, citizens can have confidence that they will not be cheated and that the wealth they create will not be taken from them—by either selfish intruders or by the government itself. This protection provides citizens with assurance that if they sow, they will be permitted to reap. When this is true, people will sow and reap abundantly, and economic progress will result.

In contrast, when the protective function is performed poorly, problems will abound. Opportunities to get ahead through deception, fraud, theft, and political favoritism rather than through production and trade will emerge. Earnings and wealth will be insecure, and market prices will fail to register the true cost of supplying goods and services. Incentives to develop resources will be weak, and economic growth will stagnate. Unfortunately, this is precisely the situation in many poor, less-developed countries.

The second primary function of government, the **productive function,** involves the provision of activities that are difficult to provide through markets. There is both an indirect and direct component of this productive function. The indirect component involves the creation of an environment for the efficient operation of markets. As noted, a legal structure that protects property rights and enforces contracts enhances gains from trade and market efficiency. Similarly, monetary arrangements that provide residents with access to money with stable purchasing power across time reduces uncertainty and facilitates gains from exchange. The provision of a stable monetary and price environment is one of the most important productive functions of government. As discussed in Part 2, Element 5, when governments perform this function well, people will invest more, cooperate more fully through trade, and achieve higher income levels.

Sometimes the productive function of government is more direct. There are some goods for which it is difficult to establish a one-to-one relationship between payment for and receipt of the good. For example, national defense is jointly consumed by the citizenry. It would be virtually impossible to provide some citizens with protection against foreign aggressors without simultaneously providing it to all. Markets will tend to produce too little of goods with such characteristics. As a result, government provision may improve economic conditions. This issue is considered in more detail in Element 3 below.

In other cases, it may be very costly to monitor usage and collect payments directly from users. When this is the case, it may be inefficient to provide such goods through markets. Roads, particularly those in cities and towns, provide an example. The cost of collecting fees and thereby charging users directly for their use would be exceedingly high. Thus, it is typically more efficient to make most roads available to all and finance them through taxation.

As we have stressed throughout, getting the most value from our resources requires that actions be undertaken only when the benefits exceed the costs. This principle applies to government as well as market activity. Unfortunately, when government action involves projects financed with taxes or through borrowing, both benefits and costs are difficult to measure. In the marketplace, the choices of buyers and sellers reveal information about benefits and costs. Consumers will not purchase goods unless they value them more than their price. Similarly, producers will not continue to supply goods unless they can cover their costs. But the information provided by the choices of consumers and producers is lost when the government undertakes an activity and finances it with taxes. There are no buyers spending their own money and thereby revealing information about their benefits. Moreover, the revenues paid to the suppliers were extracted through compulsory taxation and therefore they provide no assurance that the project is valued more than its cost.

Government planners may try to estimate the benefits and costs, but their estimates, to a large degree, will be guesses because they lack solid information based on the choices of buyers and sellers. Further, in the real world, such benefit-cost calculations will often be influenced by political considerations.

As the quote from Thomas Jefferson introducing this element indicates, it is vitally important for government to restrain people from imposing harm on others (the government's protective function). Economics also indicates that there is a case for government provision of goods that are difficult to supply through markets (the government's productive function). However, as the government moves beyond these activities, the case for still more government weakens. In order to better evaluate the economic role of government, developing a deeper understanding of the shortcomings of markets and applying the tools of economics to the operation of the political process are important.

2. *When monopoly is present and barriers to entry high, markets will fail to achieve ideal efficiency.*

If a society is going to get the most out of its resources, the resources must be used efficiently. Competition is central to this efficient use. As previously discussed, businesses operating in a competitive environment have incentives to cater to the views of consumers and produce goods and services economically. If businesses do not provide consumers with value for the price they pay, they will spend their money elsewhere.

A monopoly exists when there is a firm that is the only producer of a good or service for which there are no good substitutes. When this is the case, the firm will have an incentive to restrict output and raise price. By producing a smaller quantity and charging a higher price, the firm may be able to earn more profit than it would if resources were being used more productively—producing a larger quantity at a lower price. Inefficiency will result because the firm is failing to produce some units of the good or service that customers value more than their cost of production.

There are two major sources of monopoly: economies of scale and grants of privilege. Economies of scale occur when large firms have lower per-unit costs than their smaller rivals. If economies of scale persist as a firm obtains a larger and larger share of the market, a single firm will dominate and become a monopoly. The production of electricity provides an example. As power plants for the generation of electricity become larger, the per-unit cost of generating electricity generally declines. As a result, there is a tendency for a single, large firm to dominate this market. This is why the government usually regulates the prices charged by electric power companies and, in some cases, owns and operates the power plants.

Even where monopolies do not develop, some industries may have only a few dominant firms, usually because the market is costly to enter. A firm may have to produce a large share of the industry output—for example 20 or 25 percent—in order to achieve a low per-unit cost and compete effectively. When this is the case, there may be room for only four or five low per-unit cost firms. Such markets tend to be dominated by a small number of firms, which have an incentive to collude, raise the price of their product, and act as a monopolist would. Manufacturing industries such as automobiles, television sets, and computer operating systems are examples of markets dominated by a relatively small number of firms.

But the government itself is sometimes the source of monopoly. Licensing, taxes that favor one group over another, tariffs, quotas, and other grants of privilege reduce the competitiveness of markets. While some of these policies may be well-intentioned, they protect existing firms and make it more difficult for potential rivals to enter the market, thereby encouraging monopolies and dominant firms.

What can the government do to ensure that markets are competitive? The first guideline might be borrowed from the medical profession: Do no harm. The government should refrain from making things worse through licensing requirements and discriminatory taxes. In the vast majority of markets, sellers will find it difficult or impossible to limit the entry of rival firms (including rival producers from other countries). This means that suppliers will be unable to limit competition unless government imposes entry restrictions or creates rules and regulations that favor some firms relative to rivals.

To promote competition, governments may also prohibit anticompetitive actions such as collusion, the merger of dominant firms in an industry, and interlocking ownership of firms. In this regard, the United States has enacted a series of "antitrust" laws, most notably the Sherman Antitrust Act (1890) and the Clayton Act (1914), making it illegal for firms to collude or attempt to monopolize a market.

The record of government in this area has been mixed, however. On the one hand, government policies have reduced the incidence of collusion and various practices that limit competition. But some laws have almost the opposite effect; they restrict entry into markets, protect existing producers from rivals, and limit price competition. Thus, while high entry barriers and the absence of competition provide the potential for government to improve market performance, some policies have actually granted monopoly powers. As we proceed, the underlying reasons for this become more visible.

3. Public goods and externalities result in incentives that may encourage self-interested individuals to undertake activities that are inconsistent with ideal economic efficiency.

As we have stressed, if markets are going to allocate resources efficiently, property rights must be well-established and producers must be able to capture the benefits of their productive actions. But the nature of some goods makes this difficult. In this element, two categories of economic activity that pose serious challenges to the efficient allocation of resources through markets are considered. They are public goods and externalities.

Public Goods

The nature of some goods makes it difficult for producers to benefit from their production. This is the case with a category of goods that economists call public goods. **Public goods** have the following two characteristics: (1) jointness in consumption—provision of the good to one party simultaneously makes it available to others; and (2) nonexcludability—it is difficult or virtually impossible to exclude nonpaying customers. For example, flood control meets the first criterion because once it is provided everyone in the region benefits, and it meets the second criterion because the supplier will have trouble charging people for the service. Thus, because potential suppliers are unable to establish a one-to-one relationship between payment for and receipt of the good, it will be difficult to provide public goods through markets.

Consumers will have an incentive to become "free riders"—to consume the good even though they do not help to pay for it. And when a large number of people become free riders, the good may not be produced (or too little of it may be produced) even when the value derived from its consumption exceeds the cost. In such cases, markets will often fail to produce a quantity of public goods consistent with economic efficiency. In addition to flood control, national defense, municipal police protection, and mosquito abatement are examples of public goods. Because these goods are difficult to supply through markets, they are often provided by governments.

It is important to note that it is the characteristic of a good, not the sector in which it is produced, that determines whether it qualifies as a public good. There is a tendency to think that if a good is provided by the government, then it is a public good. This is not the case. Many of the goods provided by governments clearly do not have the characteristics of public goods. Medical services, education, mail delivery, trash collection, and electricity come to mind. Although these goods are often supplied by governments, nonpaying customers could be easily excluded and providing them to one party does not make them available to others. Thus, even though they are often provided by governments, they are not public goods.

There are very few public goods and services. In most cases it is easy to establish a link between payment and receipt of a good or service. If you do not pay for a gallon of ice cream, an automobile, television set, smart phone, a pair of jeans, and literally thousands of other items, suppliers will not provide them to you and you cannot freely benefit from those items purchased by others. In the case of private goods, it is unlikely that consumers will benefit from government provision.

Externalities

Sometimes the actions of an individual or group will "spill over" and exert an impact on others, affecting their well-being without their consent. Such spillover effects are called **externalities**. For example, if you are trying to study and others in your home or apartment complex are distracting you with loud music, they are imposing an externality on you. You are an external party—not directly involved in the transaction, activity, or exchange—but you have been affected by it, detrimentally in this case.

The spillover effects may either impose a cost or create a benefit for external parties. When the spillover effects are harmful, they are called external costs. Because costs are imposed on nonconsenting parties, resources may be used to produce goods that are valued less than their full production costs, and inefficiency results.

Consider the production of paper. The firms in the market purchase trees, labor, and other resources to first produce pulp, and then paper. The manufacturing process may emit pollutants into the atmosphere that impose costs on residents living around the mills—the smell caused by sulfur, the organic compounds that contribute to smog, and even pollutants that can cause paint on buildings to deteriorate. Such pollutants may make it difficult for some people to breathe normally and perhaps cause other health hazards.

If the residents living near a pulp mill can prove they have been harmed, they could take the mill to court and force the paper producer to cover the cost of their damages. But it will often be difficult to prove the harm and that the pulp mill is responsible. When this is the case, the costs they experience will not be reflected through markets and, therefore, the cost of producing paper will be understated. Inefficiency occurs because units of paper will be produced that are valued less than the costs of their production, including the external costs.

To a large degree, external costs reflect a lack of fully defined and enforced property rights. Because the property right to a resource— clean air for example—is poorly enforced, the firm does not pay the full cost of using the resource. Thus, the cost of producing goods and services using such resources is understated.

Sometimes the spillover effects will generate benefits for others. When the spillover effects enhance others' welfare, they are called external benefits. But external benefits can pose problems for markets, too. When the persons or firms that generate the external benefits are uncompensated, they may fail to produce some units even when they are valued more than their production costs.

For example, suppose a pharmaceutical company develops a vaccine providing protection against a deadly virus. The vaccine can easily be marketed to consumers who will benefit directly from it. However, because of the communal nature of viruses, as more and more people take the vaccine, those who haven't bought the vaccine will also be less likely to catch the virus. Yet it will be very difficult for the pharmaceutical companies to capture the benefits derived by the nonusers. As a result, they may produce too little of the vaccine. Thus, when external benefits are present, market forces may supply less than the amount consistent with economic efficiency.

Perhaps the government should take action. In the case of external costs, a tax imposed on the activities that generate the external costs might lead the person or firm to reduce its activities and achieve an output level more consistent with economic efficiency. Similarly, in the case of external benefits, government subsidies might spur production, resulting in a more efficient output level.

The potential adverse consequences of externalities can sometimes be controlled without government, however. In the case of external benefits, entrepreneurs have an incentive to figure out ways to capture more fully the gains their actions generate for others. The development of golf courses illustrates this point. Because of the beauty and openness of golf courses, many people find it attractive to live nearby. Thus, constructing a golf course typically generates an external benefit—an increase in the value of the nearby property. In recent years, golf course developers have figured out how to capture this benefit. Now, they typically purchase a large tract of land around the planned course before it is built. This lets them resell the land at a higher price after the golf course has been completed and the surrounding land has increased in value. By extending the scope of their activities to include real estate as well as golf course development, they are able to obtain revenues from what would otherwise be external benefits.

As for external costs, simple rules can help control them. For example, with respect to noise from nearby residents, apartment owners often have rules about playing loud music late at night and they enforce the rules by expelling violators. Manners and social conventions can also play a role. If your roommates are aware that having the television on interferes with your studying, they may have the good manners to turn it off. More broadly, over time it has become "socially unacceptable" for companies to emit pollution that harms people and their environment. There is increasing pressure for companies to be good citizens—and private watchdogs such as environmental groups will publicize their actions if they behave irresponsibly.

Our analysis indicates that public goods and externalities may undermine the efficient operation of markets. Economists use the term **market**

failure to describe the situation where the existing structure of incentives creates a conflict between personal self-interest and getting the most out of the available resources. Market failure encourages self-interested decision-makers to engage in counterproductive rather than productive activities.

Market failure creates the potential for government action to improve economic efficiency. But the political process is merely an alternative form of economic organization. We need to know more about how that form of organization works so that it can be compared realistically with markets.[3] We now turn to that topic.

4. Allocation through political voting is fundamentally different than market allocation.

> *The first lesson of economics is scarcity: there is never enough of anything to fully satisfy all those who want it. The first lesson of politics is to disregard the first lesson of economics.*[4]
>
> —THOMAS SOWELL, PROFESSOR OF ECONOMICS,
>
> STANFORD UNIVERSITY

The political process is an alternative form of economic organization. It is not a corrective device that can be counted on to provide a sound remedy when problems arise. Even when it is controlled by elected political

3. A. C. Pigou, who many consider to be the father of welfare economics, makes this same point. In his 1932 classic *The Economics of Welfare* (Part II, Chapter 20, Section 4), Pigou stated, "It is not sufficient to contrast the imperfect adjustments of unfettered private enterprise with the best adjustment that economists in their studies can imagine. For we cannot expect that any public authority will attain, or will even whole-heartedly seek, that ideal. Such authorities are liable alike to ignorance, to sectional pressure and to personal corruption by private interest. A loud-voiced part of their constituents, if organised for votes, may easily outweigh the whole."
4. Thomas Sowell. N.d. BrainyQuote.com. Retrieved October 17, 2015, from Brainy Quote.com:brainyquote.com/quotes/quotes/t/thomassowe371242.html.

officials (as opposed to, say, an autocratic regime), there is no assurance that government actions will be productive. This is particularly true when governments become heavily involved in allocating scarce resources toward favored sectors, businesses, and interest groups. As mentioned in the introduction to Part 3, the public choice analysis developed during the past half century provides considerable insight into the operation of democratic political decision-making.

Clearly, policies favored by a majority do not always make a society better off. Here's a thought experiment: Consider a simple economy with five voters. Suppose three of the voters favor a project that gives each a net benefit of $2, but imposes a net cost of $5 on each of the other two voters. In aggregate, the project generates net costs of $10 against net benefits of only $6. It is counterproductive and will make the five-person society worse off. Nonetheless, if decided by majority vote, it would pass three to two. Increasing the number of voters from five to 5 million or 200 million will not alter the general outcome. As this simple example illustrates, majority voting can clearly lead to adoption of counterproductive projects.

It is useful to compare markets with democratic political allocation, the major alternative form of economic organization. It is particularly important to keep the following four points in mind.

First, in a democracy, the basis for government action is majority rule. In contrast, market activity is based on mutual agreement and voluntary exchange. In a democratic setting, when a majority—either directly or through their elected representatives—adopts a policy, the minority is forced to pay for its support even if they strongly disagree. For example, if the majority votes for a new baseball stadium, housing subsidy program, or bailout of an automobile company, minority voters are forced to yield and pay taxes for support of such projects. Whether they benefit or not, they pay higher taxes, suffer loss of income, or are harmed in other ways.

The power to tax and regulate makes it possible for the majority to coerce the minority. There is no such coercive power when resources are allocated by markets. Market exchanges do not occur unless all parties agree. Private firms can charge a high price, but they cannot force anyone to buy their product. Indeed, private firms must provide benefits that exceed the price charged in order to attract customers.

Second, there is little incentive for voters to be well-informed about either candidates or issues. An individual voter will virtually never decide the outcome of an election. It is more likely that a voter will be struck by lightning on the way to the polling place than it is that their vote will be decisive in a large city, congressional, or statewide election!

Recognizing this point, most voters spend little, if any, time and energy studying issues and candidates in order to cast a well-informed vote. Most simply decide on the basis of information acquired as the result of their other activities (watching television, interaction with friends on social media, or discussions at the office). Given these incentives, most voters have little or no idea where candidates stand or what impact government actions (such as agricultural subsidies and trade restrictions) have on the economy. Economists refer to this as the **rational ignorance effect**. That is, voters are poorly informed, but their lack of information is rational because an individual's vote is so rarely decisive.

The weak incentive of voters to make informed choices is in sharp contrast to that of consumers in the marketplace. Market consumers individually decide how to spend their money, and if they make bad choices, they personally bear the consequences. That fact gives them the motivation to spend their money wisely. When consumers consider the purchase of an automobile, personal computer, gym membership, or thousands of similar items, they have a strong incentive to acquire information and make informed choices.

Third, the political process generally imposes the same outcome on everyone, while markets allow for diverse representation. Put another way, government allocation results in a "one size fits all" outcome, while markets allow different individuals and groups to "vote" for and receive desired options. This can be illustrated with schooling. When schooling is allocated through the market (through private schools and home-schooling), rather than supplied by the government, some parents choose schools that stress religious values, while others opt for education that emphasizes basic skills, cultural diversity, or vocational preparation. Individual buyers (or members of a group) willing to pay the cost are able to choose a desired educational option and receive it. Markets provide for a system of proportional representation and this makes it possible for more people to obtain goods and services more consistent with their preferences. Moreover, markets also avoid the conflicts that inevitably arise when the majority imposes its will on various minorities.

Fourth, market and political decision-makers face different incentives. As previously discussed, the profit-and-loss mechanism of a market economy tends to direct resources toward productive projects and away from counterproductive ones. But, the political process does not have a similar mechanism that can be counted on to direct resources toward productive activities. This is true even when controlled through voting. Instead, when unconstrained by constitutional limits, elected officials will tend to gain votes by providing favors to some at the expense of others. As the saying goes, if you take from Peter and give to Paul, you can usually count on the support of Paul.

To a large degree, the modern political process can be viewed as a series of "exchanges" between coalitions and politicians. Concentrated interest groups provide votes, financial contributions, high-paying jobs in the future, and other forms of support in exchange for subsidies, spending programs, and regulatory favors often financed by taxpayers. The rational ignorance effect—the fact that voters choose not to spend the time required to be well-informed—facilitates this process because a lot can happen in the halls of Congress of which voters are unaware. As a result, resources are moved toward lobbying and other favor-seeking activities and away from production and development of better products.

As explained in the two previous elements, economic analysis indicates there are cases where markets will fail to allocate resources efficiently. But this is also true of the political process. Put another way, there is government failure as well as market failure. **Government failure** is present when the incentives confronted by political participants encourage counterproductive rather than productive use of resources. Like market failure, government failure reflects the situation where there is a conflict between what is best for individual decision-makers and getting the most value out of resources.

The framers of the United States Constitution were aware that even a democratic government might undertake counterproductive actions. Thus, they incorporated restraints on the economic role of government. They enumerated the permissible taxing and spending powers of the central government (Article I, Section 8) and allocated all other powers to the states and the people (Tenth Amendment). They also prohibited states from adopting legislation "impairing the obligation of contracts" (Article I, Section 10). Furthermore, the Fifth Amendment specifies that private property shall not be "taken for public use without just compensation." Over time, however, Supreme Court decisions eroded these restraints, and government control over both individuals and businesses expanded, as did federal control over the states. As we proceed, we will analyze in more detail the operation of the democratic political process and consider modifications that might bring government into greater harmony with economic growth and prosperity.

5. Unless restrained by constitutional rules, special-interest groups will use the democratic political process to obtain government favors at the expense of others.

Democratically elected officials can often benefit by supporting policies that favor special-interest groups at the expense of the general public. Consider a policy that generates substantial personal gain for the members of a well-organized group (for example, an association representing business interests, members of a labor union, or a farm group) at the expense of the broader interests of taxpayers or consumers. While the organized interest group has fewer members than the total number of taxpayers or consumers, each member's personal gain from the legislation is likely to be large. In contrast, while many taxpayers and consumers are harmed, the cost imposed on each is small, and the source of the cost is often difficult to identify.

Since the personal stake of the interest group members is substantial, they have a powerful incentive to form alliances and let candidates and legislators know how strongly they feel about the issue. Many interest group members will decide whom to vote for and whom to support financially almost exclusively on the basis of a politician's stand on a few issues of special importance to them. In contrast, as the rational ignorance effect illustrates, the bulk of voters will be generally uninformed and they will not care much about the **special-interest issue** because each one exerts little impact on their personal welfare.

If you were a vote-seeking politician, what would you do? Clearly you would not get much campaign support by favoring the interests of the largely uninformed and unorganized majority. But you can get vocal supporters, campaign workers, and, most important, campaign contributions by favoring the position of the special interest. In the age of media politics, politicians are under strong pressure to support special interests, tap them for campaign funds, and use the contributions to project a positive candidate image on television and the Internet. Politicians unwilling to play this game—those unwilling to use the government treasury to provide well-organized interest groups with favors in exchange for political support—are seriously disadvantaged. Given these incentives, politicians are led as if by an invisible hand to reflect the views of special-interest groups, even though this often leads to policies that, summed across all voters, waste resources and reduce our living standards. Economists refer to this bias of the political process as the **special-interest effect**.

The power of special interests is further strengthened by logrolling and pork-barrel legislation. **Logrolling** is the practice of trading votes between politicians to get the necessary support to pass desired legislation. **Pork-barrel legislation** is the bundling of unrelated projects benefiting many interests into a single bill. Both logrolling and pork-barrel legislation often make it possible for counterproductive projects benefiting concentrated interests to gain legislative approval.

Exhibit 10 illustrates how pork-barrel politics and vote trading reinforce the special-interest effect and lead to the adoption of counterproductive projects. In this simple example, a five-member legislature is considering three projects: (1) a sports stadium in District A; (2) construction of an indoor rain forest in District B; and (3) subsidies for ethanol that generate benefits for the corn farmers of District C. For the residents of each district, the net benefit or cost is shown—that is, the benefit to the residents of the district minus the tax cost imposed on them. Note: The sum of the net benefits generated by each of the projects is negative. Because the total costs across all voters exceeds the benefits by $20, each project is counterproductive.

If these counterproductive projects were voted on separately, each would lose by a 4-to-1 vote because only one district would gain, and the other four would lose. However, when the projects are bundled together through either logrolling (representatives A, B, and C could agree to trade votes) or pork-barrel legislation (all three programs incorporated into a single bill), they can all pass, despite the fact that all are inefficient. This can be seen by noting that the total combined net benefit is positive for representatives A, B, and C. Given the weak incentive for voters to acquire information, those harmed by pork-barrelling and other special-interest policies are unlikely to even be aware of them. Thus, the incentive to support special-interest projects, including those that are counterproductive, is even stronger than is implied by the simple numeric example of Exhibit 10.

Market exchange is a win-win, positive-sum activity: Both trading partners expect to gain or the exchange will not occur. In contrast, "political exchange" can be a win-lose, negative-sum activity, where the voting majority gains but the minority loses more. Here, there is no assurance that the gains of the winners will exceed the losses imposed on others.

The tendency of the unrestrained political process to favor well-organized groups helps explain the presence of many programs that reduce the size of the economic pie. For example, consider the case of the roughly 20,000 American sugar growers. For many years, the price of

Exhibit 10: Trading Votes and Passing Counterproductive Legislation				
Net Benefits (+) or Costs (−) to Voters in Equal Size Districts				
Voters of District	Sports Stadium	Indoor Rainforest Project	Ethanol Subsidy	Total
A	$100	−$30	−$30	$40
B	−$30	$100	−$30	$40
C	−$30	−$30	$100	$40
D	−$30	−$30	−$30	−$90
E	−$30	−$30	−$30	−$90
Total	−$20	−$20	−$20	−$60

sugar paid by American consumers has been 50 percent to 100 percent higher than the world sugar price because of the federal government's price support program and highly restrictive quotas limiting the import of sugar. As a result of these programs, sugar growers gain about $1.7 billion, or approximately $85,000 per grower. Most of these benefits are reaped by large growers whose owners have incomes far above the national average. On the other hand, sugar consumers pay between $2.9 billion and $3.5 billion, or approximately $25 per household, in the form of higher sugar prices.[5] As a result, Americans are worse off because their resources are wasted in producing a good we are ill-suited to produce and one that could be obtained at a substantially lower cost through trade.

Nonetheless, Congress continues to support the sugar program, and it is easy to see why. Given the sizable impact on their personal wealth, it is perfectly sensible for sugar growers, particularly the large ones, to use their wealth and political clout to help politicians who support their interests. This is precisely what they do. During the most recent four-year election cycle, the sugar lobby contributed more than $16 million to candidates and political-action committees. A single firm, the American Crystal Sugar Company, gave $1.3 million to 221 members of Congress during this election cycle and spent another $1.4 million lobbying Congress. In contrast, it would be irrational for the average voter to investigate this issue or give it any significant weight when deciding for whom to vote. In fact, most voters are unaware that this program costs them money. Thus, politicians gain by continuing to subsidize the

---

5. See Jared Meyer and Preston Cooper, "Sugar Subsidies Are a Bitter Deal for American Consumers," *Economic Policies for the 21st Century at the Manhattan Institute,* Manhattan Institute (June 23, 2014). economics21.org/commentary/sugar-subsidies-are-bitter-deal-american-consumers. In recent years candy manufacturers and other major users of sugar have been moving to Canada, Mexico, and other countries where sugar can be purchased at the world market price. Illustrating our earlier discussion of trade, the import restrictions that "saved" jobs in the sugar-growing industry caused job losses in other industries, particularly those that use sugar intensely.

sugar industry even though the policy wastes resources and reduces the wealth of the nation.

One could say that the primary business of modern politics is to extract resources from the general public in order to provide favors to well-organized voting blocs in a manner that will create a voting majority. Examples abound. Taxpayers and consumers spend approximately $20 billion annually to support grain, cotton, tobacco, peanut, wool, and dairy programs, all of which have a structure similar to the sugar program. The political power of special interests also explains the presence of tariffs and quotas on steel, shoes, textiles, and many other products. Federally funded irrigation projects, banking bailouts, and subsidies to sports stadiums, sugar and ethanol producers, and airports in specific districts—the list goes on and on—are all policies politically motivated by the special-interest effect rather than the net benefits to Americans. While each of these programs imposes only a small drag on our economy, together they expand the federal budget, waste resources, and significantly lower our standard of living.

The special-interest effect also tends to stifle innovation and the competitive process. Older, more established businesses have built a stronger record of political contributions, have better knowledge of lobbying techniques, and have developed a closer relationship with powerful political figures. Predictably, the more mature firms will generally have more political clout than newer upstarts, and they will use it to deter innovative rivals.

Consider the experience of Uber, which uses technology to bring willing drivers together with potential ground-transportation passengers. Consumers searching for ground transportation request cars via their smartphones and the Uber app immediately gives them a wait time. Uber also provides feedback information about drivers to potential passengers and vice versa. The technology reduces transaction costs and the process is often faster and cheaper than traditional taxi service.

As Uber has sought to enter markets in large cities throughout the world, the traditional taxi industry has fought for and often achieved legislation prohibiting the use of the technology employed by Uber and similar firms seeking to enter this market.[6] As a result, the gains from the innovative technology and expansion in the volume of exchange have been slowed.

The experience of Tesla, an electric car manufacturer, provides another example of existing producers using the political process to deter the entry of a newcomer. Tesla's business model was based on the sale of its autos directly to consumers. But a well-organized interest group, the established auto dealers, lobbied state legislatures demanding that they adopt laws prohibiting manufacturers from selling their cars directly to consumers. Approximately half of the states adopted prohibitions on such direct sales. These laws made it much more difficult for Tesla to enter the auto manufacturing market.

Interestingly, the development of Tesla itself was based on government favoritism. Tesla received hundreds of millions of dollars in subsidies (grants, government guaranteed loans, and tax credits) from the federal government to develop and produce its Model S luxury electric car, which sells for more than $100,000. In 2014, the state of Nevada provided Tesla with a package of subsidies estimated to be worth $1.3 billion to build a battery-manufacturing facility near Reno. Tesla will not have to pay any payroll or property taxes for ten years and no sales taxes for twenty years, and will receive $195 million in "transferable tax credits" that can be sold to other companies to satisfy their Nevada tax bills.[7]

---

6. See Holman W. Jenkins Jr., "How Uber Won the Big Apple." *Wall Street Journal,* July 24, 2015. www.wsj.com/articles/how-uber-won-the-big-apple-1437778176.
7. See Steven Chapman. "State Laws Keep Tesla from Selling Cars," *Chicago Tribune,* June 20, 2013. articles.chicagotribune.com/2013-06-20/news/ct-oped-0620-chapman -20130620_1_tesla-motors-car-dealers-car-costs; John Voelcker, "Where Can Tesla Legally Sell Cars Directly To You? State-By-State Map: LATEST UPDATE." *Green Car Reports,* April 22, 2015, n.p. www.greencarreports.com/news/1095337_where-can

Perhaps there is a lesson here: Crony businesses that live by government favoritism will sometimes get gored by other crony businesses with even more political clout.

The framers of the Constitution of the United States were well aware of the problems arising from the power of special-interest groups. They called the interest groups "factions." The Constitution sought to limit pressure from the factions in Article I, Section 8, which specifies that Congress is to levy only uniform taxes for programs that promote the common defense and general welfare. This clause was designed to preclude the use of general tax revenue to provide benefits to subgroups of the population. However, through the years court decisions and legislative acts have altered its meaning. Thus, as it is currently interpreted, the Constitution now fails to constrain the political power of well-organized special-interest groups.

6. Unless restrained by constitutional rules, legislators will run budget deficits and spend excessively.

> *The attractiveness of financing spending by debt issue to the elected politicians should be obvious. Borrowing allows spending to be made that will yield immediate political payoffs without the incurring of any immediate political cost.*[8]

—JAMES BUCHANAN, 1986 NOBEL LAUREATE

When a government's spending exceeds its revenues, a budget deficit results. Governments generally issue interest-earning bonds to finance

---

-tesla-legally-sell-cars-directly-to-you-state-by-state-map; Phil Kerpen, "Tesla and Its Subsidies." *National Review Online,* January 26, 2015, n.p. www.nationalreview.com /article/397162/tesla-and-its-subsidies-phil-kerpen.

8. James Buchanan, *The Deficit and American Democracy* (Memphis: P. K. Steidman Foundation, 1984).

their budget deficits. These bonds comprise the national debt. An annual budget deficit increases the size of the national debt by the amount of the deficit. In contrast, when government revenues exceed spending, a budget surplus is present. This allows the government to pay off bond-holders and thereby reduce the size of its outstanding debt. Basically, the national debt represents the cumulative effect of all the prior budget deficits and surpluses.

Prior to 1960 almost everyone—including the leading figures of the major political parties—thought that the government should balance its budget except perhaps during war. There was a widespread implicit agreement—much like a constitutional rule—that the federal budget should be balanced. Except during war, both deficits and surpluses were small relative to the size of the economy.

The Keynesian revolution changed all of this. The English economist John Maynard Keynes (pronounced "canes") developed a theory that provided both an explanation for the length and severity of the Great Depression and a remedy for prevention of such events in the future. During the 1940s and 1950s, the Keynesian view swept the economics profession and it soon dominated the thinking of intellectual and political leaders. According to Keynesian analysis, government spending and budget deficits could be used to promote a more stable economy. Keynesians argued that rather than balancing the budget, the government should run budget deficits during periods of recession and shift toward a budget surplus when there was concern about inflation.

While the effectiveness of Keynesian fiscal policy is a point of controversy, its impact on the federal budget is clear. Freed from the balanced budget constraint, politicians consistently spent more than they were willing to tax. During the fifty-five years since 1960, the federal government has run fifty-one deficits and four surpluses. Exhibit 11 shows the path of the federal deficit measured as a share of GDP during this era. While the deficits have been larger during recessions, perpetual deficits have been the norm. The federal deficit averaged about 2 percent of GDP between 1960 and 1980 and the figure was even larger during the 1980s. The deficits were smaller during the 1990s and surpluses were even achieved from 1998 to 2000. But the era of deficit control was exceedingly short. The surpluses quickly evaporated and deficits soared to new highs, reaching 10 percent of GDP during the recession of 2009–2010.

Deficits push the national debt upward. Measured as a share of GDP, the outstanding federal debt has risen from 58 percent in 2000 to 70 percent in 2008, and 105 percent in 2014. The federal debt as a share of GDP now stands at the highest level since the period immediately following World War II.

The political attractiveness of spending financed by borrowing rather than taxation is not surprising. It reflects what economists call the **shortsightedness effect:** the tendency of elected political officials to favor projects that generate immediate, highly visible benefits at the expense of costs that can be cast into the future and are difficult to identify. Legislators have an incentive to spend money on programs that benefit the voters of their district and special-interest groups that will help them

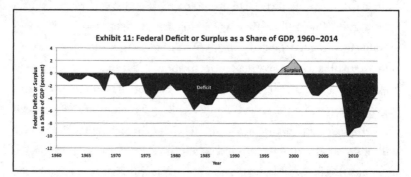

Source: Office of Management and Budget, President's Budget FY 2011 Budget, Table 1.3. www.whitehouse.gov/omb/budget/historicals/.

win reelection. They do not like to tax because taxes impose a visible cost on voters. Debt is an alternative to current taxes; it pushes the visible cost of government into the future. Budget deficits and borrowing allow politicians to supply voters with immediate benefits without imposing higher taxes. Thus, deficits are a natural outgrowth of democratic politics unrestrained by commitment to a balanced budget.

The unconstrained political process plays into the hands of well-organized interest groups and encourages politicians to increase spending to gain benefits for a few at the expense of many. For example, each member of Congress has a strong incentive to fight hard for expenditures beneficial to his or her constituents. In contrast, there is little incentive for a legislator to be a spending "watchdog" for two reasons. First, such a watchdog would incur the wrath of colleagues because the spending restraint would make it more difficult for them to deliver special programs for their districts. They would retaliate by providing little support for spending in the watchdog's district. Second, and more importantly, the benefits of spending cuts and deficit reductions that the watchdog is trying to attain (for example, lower taxes) will accrue equally to voters in the other 434 districts. Thus, even if the watchdog is successful, the constituents in his or her district will reap only a small fraction of the benefits.

Perhaps the following illustration will help explain why it is so difficult for the 435 representatives and 100 senators in Congress to bring federal spending and the budget deficit under control. Suppose these 535 individuals go out to dinner knowing that after the meal each will receive a bill for 1/535th of the cost. No one feels compelled to order less because his or her restraint will exert little impact on the total bill. Why not order shrimp for an appetizer, entrees of steak and lobster, and a large piece of cheesecake for dessert? After all, the extra spending will add only a few pennies to each person's share of the total bill. For example, if one member of the dinner party orders expensive items that push up the total bill by $50, his share of the cost will be less than 10 cents (1/535th of $50). What a bargain! Of course, he will have to pay extra for the extravagant orders of the other 534 diners, too. But that's true no matter what he orders. The result is that everyone ends up ordering extravagantly and paying more for extras that provide little value relative to cost.[9]

The incentive structure outlined here explains why deficit finance is so attractive to politicians. During the seven-year period 2008–2014, federal deficits pushed up the national debt by almost 50 percentage points as a share of GDP. Moreover, the future benefits promised to senior citizens under the Social Security and Medicare programs are far greater than the payroll tax revenues that provide their financing. These unfunded liabilities are another form of debt. In fact, the debt implied by the unfunded Social Security and Medicare liabilities is almost four times the size of the official national debt. As the baby-boomers move into the retirement phase of life, spending on Social Security and Medicare will outstrip the revenues for their finance, further complicating the debt liability of the federal government.

What will happen if the federal government does not bring its finances under control? As a nation's debt gets larger and larger relative to the size of its economy, there will be repercussions in credit markets. Extending loans to the government of a country with a large ratio of debt to GDP is risky. As a result, the highly indebted government will have to pay higher interest rates. In turn, the higher interest costs will make it even more difficult for the government to keep within its budget and keep taxes at reasonable levels.

9. We are indebted to E. C. Pasour Jr., longtime professor of economics at North Carolina State University, for this example.

If the debt continues to rise relative to income, investors will become more and more reluctant to buy the bonds issued by the United States Treasury. Eventually a financial crisis will result—either outright default by the government or financing the debt by money creation and inflation. In either case, there will be a destructive impact on the economy. This has occurred in other countries, such as Greece, that have failed to control government finances. The United States is not immune to the laws of economics.

It is vitally important for the federal government to control its spending and borrowing in the years ahead. This is unlikely to happen without a change in the political rules to make it more difficult for politicians to spend more than they are willing to tax. There are several ways this might be done. The Constitution could be amended to require the federal government to balance its budget, as most state governments are required to do. Or a constitutional amendment could require two-thirds or three-fourths approval by both houses of Congress for spending proposals and increases in the federal government's borrowing power. Or the current year's spending might be limited to last year's level of revenues. Proposed constitutional rule changes of this kind would make it more difficult for legislators to spend unless they were willing to tax or to charge users for the government services.

7. *When governments become heavily involved in providing favors to some at the expense of others, inefficiency results and improper, unethical relationships develop between government officials and businesses.*

> *The tool of politics (which frequently becomes its objective) is to extract resources from the general taxpayer with minimum offense and to distribute the proceeds among innumerable claimants in such a*

way to maximize the support at the polls. Politics, so far as mobilizing support is concerned, represents the art of calculated cheating or, more precisely, how to cheat without being caught.[10]

—JAMES R. SCHLESINGER, FORMER SECRETARY OF DEFENSE

There are two ways individuals can acquire wealth: production and plunder. People can get ahead by producing goods or services of value and exchanging them for income. This positive-sum method of acquiring income helps both trading partners and enhances the wealth of society. But sometimes people will try to get ahead through plunder, the taking from others without their consent. Of course, the victims of plunder will lose what the plunderer gains. But, in addition, where plunder is feared, potential victims will employ resources to defend themselves against it. In a society in which burglary is common, for example, people will buy more locks, use more security services, demand more police, and even design their homes in ways to discourage theft. The costs imposed on the citizenry will be greater than the gains obtained by those engaging in plunder. In contrast with positive-sum exchange activities, plunder is a negative-sum activity. It not only fails to generate additional income but also consumes resources, reducing the wealth of the society.

Governments promote economic prosperity when they encourage production and exchange, and discourage plunder. When effective law and its enforcement make it difficult to take from others, either via crime or use of political action, few resources will flow into plunder. Moreover, the resources employed defending against plunder will also be small.

In the modern world, however, government itself has become a major source of plunder. Governments often take resources from some in order

10. James R. Schlesinger, "Systems Analysis and the Political Process," *Journal of Law & Economics* (October 1968): 281.

to provide subsidies and favors to others. While it is not technically theft because it is done through laws, it is still a negative-sum activity that harms the citizenry and slows economic growth.

In the United States, transfers and subsidies now account for approximately half of the federal budget. Social Security and healthcare subsidies comprise the bulk of the transfers, but there are now more than 2,300 federal subsidy programs, up from 1,425 in 2000.[11] Numerous activities are subsidized, including irrigation of arid lands, ethanol-enriched gasoline, mortgage loans, export of aircraft, small business start-ups, production of wind and solar power, construction of low-cost housing, and production of agricultural goods ranging from corn and cotton to peanuts and wheat—to list just a few.

Subsidies and government favoritism are a danger to both political democracy and economic efficiency. There are several reasons why this is the case.

First, the subsidies distort prices and encourage businesses to spend more time searching for favoritism in Washington and less time developing better and more economical products. Predictably, an increase in the availability of government favoritism will strengthen the power of special interests and encourage deception. In order to obtain more government funds and gain advantages relative to rivals, businesses and other favor-seekers will tie their interests to popular objectives such as increasing employment, reducing poverty, improving environmental quality, and lessening dependence on foreigners. Even when their actions are motivated by financial gain and political power, interest groups will have a strong incentive to claim they are seeking to achieve broader, more popular objectives than is actually the case.

---

11. See Chris Edwards, "Why the Federal Government Fails." *Policy Analysis*, Cato Institute, No. 777 (2015): 5. object.cato.org/sites/cato/org/files/pubs/pdf/pa777.pdf.

Second, subsidies to some firms and sectors place others at a disadvantage. Some of the unsubsidized firms will be driven out of business or fail to enter the market because they can't compete with subsidized rivals. The result is a diversion of resources from businesses dependent on market consumers to those favored by politicians.

Third, and perhaps most important, the subsidies and favoritism will create an improper, unethical relationship between business and political officials. "Corporate welfare" and "crony capitalism" are thereby encouraged, and the interests of the taxpayer compromised. The greater the degree of corporate welfare (i.e., the more numerous the government subsidy programs directed toward business), the greater the flow of resources into favor-seeking activities. (Note: Economists often use the term **rent-seeking** to describe the favor seeking of businesses and other groups.) As politics replaces markets, the economy will be increasingly characterized by cronyism and counterproductive activities, and economic growth will fall below its potential.

Increasingly, the governments of the United States and other high-income democratic countries use taxes and borrowing to provide subsidies and other favors to specified voting blocs in exchange for political contributions and support. In a statement widely attributed to Scotsman Alexander Tytler, he argues:

> *A democracy cannot exist as a permanent form of government. It can only exist until the voters discover that they can vote themselves largesse from the public treasury. From that moment on, the majority always votes for the candidates promising the most benefits from the public treasury with the result that a democracy always collapses over loose fiscal policy. . . .* [12]

12. Others attribute this statement to Lord Thomas Macaulay. The author cannot be verified with certainty. For additional information on this topic, see Loren Collins, "The Truth About Tytler" at: www.lorencollins.net/tytler.html.

Once businesses and other interest groups become heavily involved in providing politicians with support in exchange for subsidies and favoritism, these forces will be very difficult to restrain. As government favoritism grows and both the recipients and politicians become more dependent on it, transfer spending will grow and resources will move away from productive activities. Moreover, deceitful behavior, unethical relations, and even corruption will become commonplace. There will be upward pressure on taxes, budget deficits will expand even further, and the politically manipulated economy will stagnate. Unless the constitutional protection of property rights and limitations on the spending, subsidizing, and borrowing activities of government are restored, democratically elected politicians will continue to enact programs that waste resources and impair the general standard of living. As illustrated by the case of Greece—whose government overspent itself into a debt crisis in 2015—this path will eventually lead to excessive debt and economic collapse.

8. *The net gain of transfer recipients is less, and often substantially less, than the amount of the transfer.*

To noneconomists, income transfers look like an effective way to help targeted beneficiaries. However, economic analysis indicates that it is actually quite difficult to transfer income to a group of recipients in a way that will improve their long-term well-being. As is often the case in economics, the unintended secondary effects explain why this proposition is true.[13]

Three major factors undermine the effectiveness of income transfers. While the process may be most vivid in the case of direct income transfers like welfare assistance, the same types of forces occur when the benefits are agricultural subsidies or grants to individuals or corporations.

---

13. See James Gwartney and Richard Stroup, "Transfers, Equality, and the Limits of Public Policy," *Cato Journal* (Spring/Summer 1986), for a detailed analysis of this issue.

First, an increase in government transfers will generally reduce the incentive of both the taxpayer-donor and the transfer recipient to earn. Many transfer programs provide for an inverse relationship between the size of the transfer and the income level of the recipient. As income rises, the magnitude of the transfer is reduced. When this is the case, neither taxpayers nor transfer recipients will produce and earn as much as they would in the absence of the transfer program. As taxes go up to finance more transfers, taxpayers have less incentive to make the sacrifices needed to produce and earn, and more incentive to invest in tax shelters to try to hang on to money earned. As for the recipients, they will have less incentive to earn because additional earnings will increase their net income by only a fraction—and in many cases only a small fraction—of the additional earnings. As a result, economic growth will be slowed.

To see the negative effect of almost any transfer policy on productive effort, consider the reaction of students if a professor announces at the beginning of the term that the grading policy for the class will redistribute the points earned on the exams so that no one will receive less than a C. Under this plan, students who earned A grades by scoring an average of 90 percent or higher on the exams would have to give up enough of their points to bring up the average of those who would otherwise get Ds and Fs. And, of course, the B students would also have to contribute some of their points as well, although not as many, in order to achieve a more equal grade distribution.

Does anyone doubt that at least some of the students who would have made As and Bs will study less when their extra effort is "taxed" to provide benefits to others? And so would the students who would have made Cs and Ds, since the penalty they paid for less effort would be cushioned by point transfers they would lose if they earned more points on their own. The same logic applies even to those who would have made Fs, although they probably weren't doing very much studying anyway. Predictably, the outcome will be less studying, and overall achievement will decline.

The impact of tax-transfer schemes will be similar: less work effort and lower overall income levels. Income is not like "manna from heaven." Instead, it is something that people produce and earn. Individuals earn income as they provide goods and services to others willing to pay for them. We can think of national income as an economic pie, but it is a pie whose size is determined by the actions of millions of people, each using production and trade to earn an individual slice. It is impossible to redistribute portions of the slices they earn without simultaneously reducing the work effort and innovative actions that generate the income.

Second, competition for transfers will erode most of the long-term gain of the intended beneficiaries. Governments must establish a criterion for the receipt of income transfers and other political favors. If they did not do so, the transfers would bust the budget immediately. Generally, the government will require a transfer recipient to own something, do something, or be something. For example, the recipient of unemployment pay must be out of a job, and a company must not have too many employees if it is to qualify for a small-business grant or loan. However, once the criterion is established, people will modify their behavior to qualify for the "free" money or other government favors. As they do so, their net gain from the transfers declines.

Think about the following. Suppose that the United States government decided to give away a $100 bill between 9:00 a.m. and 5:00 p.m. each weekday to all persons willing to wait in line at the teller windows of the United States Treasury Department. Long lines would emerge. How long? How much time would people be willing to take from their leisure and their productive activities? A person whose time was worth $10 per hour would be willing to spend almost as much as ten hours waiting in line for the $100 bill. But it might take longer than ten hours if there were enough others whose time was worth less, say $8 or $5 per hour. And everyone would find that the waiting consumed much of the value of the $100 transfer. If the proponents thought the program would make the recipients $100 better off, they would have been wrong.

This example illustrates why the intended beneficiaries of transfer programs are not helped as much as is generally perceived. When beneficiaries have to do something (for example, wait in line, fill out forms, lobby government officials, take an exam, endure delays, or contribute to selected political campaigns) in order to qualify for a transfer, often much of their potential gain will be lost as they seek to meet the qualifying criteria. Similarly, when beneficiaries have to own something (for example, land with a wheat production history to gain access to wheat program subsidies or a license to operate a taxicab or sell a product to foreigners) in order to get a subsidy, people will bid up the price of the asset needed to acquire the subsidy. The higher price of the asset, such as the taxicab license or the land with a history of wheat production, will capture the value of the subsidy.

In each case the potential beneficiaries will compete to meet the criteria until they dissipate much of the value of the transfer. As a result, the recipient's net gain will generally be substantially less than the amount of the transfer payment. Indeed, the net gain of the marginal recipient (the person who barely finds it worthwhile to qualify for the transfer) will be very close, if not equal, to zero.

Consider the impact of the subsidies (grants and low-cost loans) to college students. These programs were designed to make college more affordable. But the subsidies increase the demand for college, which pushes tuition prices upward. A recent study by the Federal Reserve Bank of New York estimates that about 65 percent of the increases in transfers to students is passed through in the form of higher tuition prices. Put another way, for every $3 increase in student subsidies, colleges and universities raise tuition by $2.[14] It is no coincidence that as the grant and loan aid programs for college students have increased substantially during the past two decades, so, too, has college tuition. Furthermore, the subsidy programs have contributed to a glut of college students entering the job market, which has reduced their employment prospects as well as the value of their degrees. When the secondary effects on both tuition costs and employment opportunities are taken into consideration, it is clear that the net benefits to college students are substantially less than the transfers.

Transfer programs can even leave intended beneficiaries worse off. The Homestead Act of 1862 illustrates this point. Under this legislation, the federal government provided a land plot of 160 acres (later expanded to up to 640 acres in parts of the West) to settlers who staked a claim, built a house on the land, and stayed for five years. This option attracted many, but it was not easy to survive in the early West, even with 160 acres. Thus, more than 60 percent of the land claims were abandoned before the five years lapsed.[15] In essence, this transfer program encouraged people to settle the land before it was economical to do so, and many of the homesteaders made a heavy sacrifice trying to qualify for this subsidy.

More recently, as discussed in Part 2, government regulations designed to make housing more affordable encouraged lenders to extend more loans with little or no down payment to homebuyers who could not qualify for conventional mortgage loans. The impact of these regulatory subsidies was much like those of the Homestead Act: high default rates,

14. See David O. Lucca, Taylor Nadauld, and Karen Shen, "Credit Supply and the Rise in College Tuition: Evidence from the Expansion in Federal Student Aid Programs." *Federal Reserve Bank of New York Staff Reports,* No. 733 (July 2015). www.newyorkfed .org/research/staff_reports/sr733.pdf.
15. Fred A. Shannon, "The Homestead Act and the Labor Surplus," *American Historical Review* (July 1936) 41: 637–51

foreclosures, and financial troubles for many of the intended beneficiaries.

There is a third reason for the ineffectiveness of transfers. Transfer programs reduce the adverse consequences suffered by those who make imprudent decisions, and this reduces their motivation to take steps to avoid the adversity. For example, government subsidies of insurance premiums in areas prone to hurricanes reduce the personal cost of individuals protecting themselves against economic losses resulting from hurricanes. But there is a cost to society. Because the subsidy makes the purchase of hurricane insurance cheaper, more people will build in hurricane-prone areas, which results in hurricanes doing more damage than they would otherwise. Unemployment compensation provides another example. The benefits make it less costly for unemployed workers to refuse existing offers and keep looking for better jobs. Therefore, workers spend longer time periods searching for jobs, which makes the unemployment rate higher than would otherwise be the case.[16]

Often, the combination of these secondary effects is present. The War on Poverty provides a clear example. When the War on Poverty was declared in the mid-1960s, President Lyndon Johnson and other proponents of the program argued that poverty could be eliminated if only Americans were willing to transfer a little more income to the less fortunate members of society. They were willing, and income-transfer programs expanded substantially. Measured as a proportion of total income, transfers directed toward the poor or near poor (for example, Aid to Families with Dependent Children, food stamps, and Medicaid) doubled during

---

16. For evidence on this point, see Lawrence Katz and Bruce Meyer, "The Impact of the Potential Duration of Unemployment Benefits on the Duration of Unemployment," *Journal of Public Economics* 41, No. 1 (February 1990): 45–72. Also see Daniel Aaronson, Bhashkar Mazumder, and Shani Schechter, "What Is Behind the Rise in Long-Term Unemployment?" Federal Reserve Bank of Chicago, *Economic Perspectives* (Second Quarter 2010): 28–51.

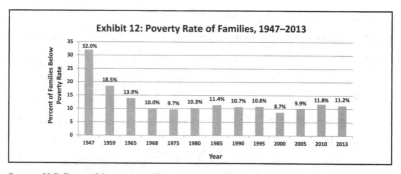

Source: U.S. Dept. of Commerce, *Characteristics of the Population Below the Poverty Level: 1982*, Table 5; and U.S. Census Bureau, Historical Poverty Tables—Families, www.census.gov/hhes/www/poverty/histpov/hstpov4.xls.

the 1965–1975 period. Since 1975, anti-poverty income transfers have continued to grow as a share of national income.

No doubt, the proponents of the War on Poverty programs were motivated by lofty objectives. However, as we have stressed, good intentions do not guarantee the desired outcome. As Exhibit 12 shows, the poverty rate was declining rapidly prior to the War on Poverty. The share of families in poverty declined from 32 percent in 1947 to 13.9 percent in 1965. The downward trend continued for a few more years, reaching 10 percent in 1968. In the late 1960s, only a few years after the War on Poverty transfers were initiated, the declining trend in the poverty rate came to a halt. Since 1970, the poverty rate of families has fluctuated within a relatively narrow range between 10 percent and 12 percent. In 2013, the poverty rate was 11.2 percent, virtually the same as the figure when the War on Poverty programs were initiated.[17] Given that income per person, adjusted for inflation, has more than doubled since the late 1960s, this lack of progress is startling.

17. The calculation of the official poverty rate does not include noncash benefits such as those of food, health care, and housing. If noncash benefits were counted as income, the family poverty rate would be about 3 percentage points lower. However, the pattern is still the same as that of Exhibit 12. When noncash benefits are counted as income, the family poverty rate in 2013 is still almost the same as in 1970.

Why haven't the anti-poverty transfer programs been more effective? The transfers generate three unintended secondary effects that slow progress against poverty.

First, the income-linked transfers reduce the incentive of low-income individuals to earn, move up the income ladder, and escape poverty. There are at least seventy-five means-tested government programs (for example, food stamps, Medicaid, housing subsidies, school lunches, and child healthcare insurance) that target the poor for assistance. Individuals are eligible to receive benefits under these programs as long as their income is at or below a designated income level. The benefits from most of these programs are scaled down and eventually eliminated as the recipients' earnings rise.

As a result, many low-income recipients get caught in a poverty trap. If they earn more, their transfer benefits are reduced and the combination of the additional taxes owed and transfers lost means that they get to keep only 10, 20, or 30 percent of the additional earnings. In some cases, the additional earnings may even reduce the recipient's net income. Thus, the poverty trap substantially reduces the incentive for many low-income recipients to work, earn more, acquire experience, and move up the job ladder. Hence, to a large degree, the transfers merely replace income that would have otherwise been earned, and as a result, the net gains of the poor are small—far less than the transfer spending suggests.

Second, transfer programs that significantly reduce the hardship of poverty also reduce the opportunity cost of risky choices such as dropping out of school or the workforce, childbearing by teenagers and unmarried women, divorce, abandonment of children by fathers, and drug use that often lead to poverty. As more people choose these high-risk options, it is very difficult to reduce the poverty rate. The poverty rate of single-parent households is approximately five times the rate for two-parent households. Today, nearly 30 percent of children live in single-parent families, up from 12 percent in 1968. Further, slightly more than 40 percent of children are now born to unwed mothers. A 2009 study by Isabel Sawhill and Ron Haskins of the Brookings Institution found that a person can reduce his or her chances of living in poverty from 12 percent to 2 percent by doing just three basic things: completing high school (at a minimum), working full time, and getting married before having a child.[18] When young people choose these options, it is unlikely that they will spend any significant time in poverty. This is a vitally important point that educators, parents, guardians, and others need to discuss with young people, many of whom are making these life-changing decisions.

Third, government antipoverty transfers crowd out private charitable efforts. When people perceive that the government is providing for the poor, action by families, churches, and civic organizations becomes less urgent. When taxes are levied and the government does more, predictably, private individuals and groups will do less. Further, private givers are more likely to see the real nature of the problem, be more sensitive to the lifestyles of recipients, and focus their giving on those making a good effort to help themselves. As a result, private charitable efforts will tend to be more effective than those of the government, and therefore the problem worsens as the private efforts are crowded out.

From an economic viewpoint, the poor record of transfer programs ranging from farm price supports to antipoverty programs is not surprising. When the secondary effects are considered, economic analysis indicates that it is extremely difficult to help the intended beneficiaries over the long term.

---

18. Ron Haskins and Isabel V. Sawhill, *Opportunity Society* (Washington, D.C.: Brookings Institution Press, 2009).

9. The economy is far too complex to be centrally planned and efforts to do so will result in inefficiency and cronyism.

The man of system is apt to be very wise in his own conceit. He seems to imagine that he can arrange the different members of a great society with as much ease as the hand arranges the different pieces upon a chess-board; he does not consider that the pieces upon the chess-board have no other principle of motion besides that which the hand impresses upon them; but that, in the great chess-board of human society, every single piece has a principle of motion of its own, although different from that which the legislature might choose to impress upon it. If those two principles coincide and act in the same direction, the game of human society will go on easily and harmoniously, and is very likely to be happy and successful. If they are opposite or different, the game will go on miserably, and the society must be at all times in the highest degree of disorder.[19]

—ADAM SMITH (1759), *THE THEORY OF MORAL SENTIMENTS*

As previously discussed, governments can often coordinate the provision of public goods—a small class of goods for which it is difficult to limit consumption to paying customers—better than markets. Many people also believe that government officials can manage all, or most, of the economy better than markets. The proponents of central planning believe that the general populace would be better off if government officials used taxes, subsidies, mandates, directives, and regulations to centrally plan and manage the key sectors of the economy. Central plan-

19. Adam Smith, *The Theory of Moral Sentiments,* Glasgow Edition of Oxford University Press (Indianapolis: Liberty Fund, Inc., [1790] 1976): 233–34. Also available at: www.econlib.org/library/Smith,smMS6.html#VI.II.42.

ning replaces markets with government. It can involve direct command and control, as under the old Soviet system. But it can also occur when elected political officials substitute their verdicts for those of consumers, investors, and entrepreneurs directed by market forces.

It is easy to see why central planning has a certain appeal to the novice. Surely it makes sense to plan. Aren't elected officials and government experts more likely to represent the "general welfare" of the people than business entrepreneurs? Won't government officials be "less greedy" than private businesses? People who do not understand public choice economics and the operation of the political process often find the argument for central planning persuasive. Economics, however, indicates that central planning will be inefficient. There are five major reasons why this will be the case.

First, central planning merely substitutes politics for market decisions. Real-world central planners (and the legislators who direct them) are not a group of omniscient selfless saints. Inevitably, the subsidies and investment funds allocated by planners will be influenced by political considerations. Think how this process works even when decisions are made democratically.

Expenditures will have to be approved by the legislature. Various business and unionized labor interests will lobby for investment funds and subsidies. Legislators will be particularly sensitive to those in a position to provide campaign contributions or to deliver key voting blocs. Predictably, the political process will favor older firms with more lobbying experience and political clout, even if they are economically weak, over newer growth-oriented firms. In addition, the chairmen of key congressional committees will often block various programs unless other legislators agree to support projects beneficial to their constituents and favored interest groups ("pork-barrel" projects). Given this incentive structure, only a naïve idealist would expect this politicized process to result in less waste, more wealth creation, and a better allocation of investment funds than markets.

Second, the incentive of government enterprises and agencies to keep costs low, be innovative, and efficiently supply goods is weak. Unlike private owners, the directors and managers of public-sector enterprises have little to gain from improved efficiency and lower costs. Rather than serving customers to build their agencies, they rely on a government budget. Predictably, they will be motivated to pursue a larger budget. A larger budget will provide funding for expansion, salary increases, additional spending on clients, and other factors that will make life more comfortable for the managers. Managers of government enterprises and agencies, almost without exception, will try to convince the planners that their activities are producing goods or services that are enormously valuable to the general public and, if they were just given more funds, they would do even more marvelous things for society. Moreover, they will argue, if the funding is not forthcoming, people will suffer and the consequences will likely be disastrous.

It will often be difficult for legislators and other government planners to evaluate such claims. There is nothing comparable to private-sector profit that the planners can use to measure performance of the enterprise managers. In the private sector, bankruptcy eventually weeds out inefficient producers, but in the public sector, there is no parallel mechanism for the termination of unsuccessful programs. In fact, poor performance and failure to achieve objectives is often used as an argument for increased government funding. For example, the police department will use a rising crime rate to argue for additional law-enforcement funding. Similarly, if the achievement scores of students are declining, public school administrators will use this failure to argue for still more funds. Given the strong incentive of government enterprise managers to expand their budgets, and the weak incentive to operate efficiently, government enterprises can be expected to have higher per-unit costs than comparable private firms.

Third, there is every reason to believe that investors risking their own money will make better investment choices than central planners spending the money of taxpayers. Remember, an investor who is going to profit must discover and invest in a project that increases the value of resources. The investor who makes a mistake—that is, whose project results in losses—will bear the consequences directly. In contrast, the success or failure of government projects seldom exerts much impact on the personal wealth of government planners. Even if a project is productive, the planner's personal gain is likely to be modest. Similarly, if the project is wasteful—if it reduces the value of resources—this failure will exert little negative impact on the income of planners. They may even be able to reap personal gain from wasteful projects that channel subsidies and other benefits toward politically powerful groups who will then give their agency or enterprise added political support. Given this incentive structure, there is no reason to believe that government planners will be more likely than private investors to discover and act on projects that increase society's wealth.

Fourth, the efficiency of government spending will also be undermined because the budget of an unconstrained government is something like a common pool resource. As we saw in Part 2, Element 1, private ownership provides a strong motivation to take the future effects of current decisions into consideration. But when money and resources are owned in common there is little motivation to consider the future. For example, fish in the ocean are owned in common until someone catches them and, as a result, many species are on the verge of depletion because of overfishing. All fishermen would be better off if the fish were harvested less rapidly so there would be more opportunity for their populations to reproduce. But, because of the common ownership, each fisherman knows that fish he does not catch today will be caught by someone else tomorrow. Thus, there is little incentive for anyone to reduce his or her catch today so more fish will be available in the future.

Similarly, when interest groups are "fishing" (that is, lobbying political planners) for government spending, they have little incentive to consider the adverse consequences of higher taxes and additional borrowing on future output. The proponents of each spending project may recognize that future output would be greater if taxes were lower and private investment higher. But they will also recognize that if they do not grab more of the government budget, some other interest group will. Given these incentives, inefficient spending projects and perpetual budget deficits are an expected result. See the discussion in Part 3, Element 6, on the problem of chronic government budget deficits.

Fifth, there is no way that central planners can acquire enough information to create, maintain, and constantly update a plan that makes sense. We live in a world of dynamic change. Technological advances, new products, political unrest, changing demand, and shifting weather conditions are constantly altering the relative scarcity of both goods and resources. No central authority will be able to keep up with these changes, politically assess them, and provide enterprise managers with sensible instructions.

Markets are different. Market prices register and tabulate widely fragmented information. Price information is constantly adjusting to reflect the persistent changes taking place in the economy. Prices reflect this widely dispersed information and send signals to business firms and resource suppliers. These price signals provide businesses and resource owners with the information—and the incentives—required to coordinate their actions and bring them into harmony with the new conditions. Failure to properly interpret these market price signals and respond properly will bring losses to the business or individuals.

It is the information communicated through market prices that informs investors, firms, and workers where their dollars and efforts create the most value for others. Without market prices for their output, government agencies make decisions without any such parallel measure of whether they are creating positive net values or wasting resources.

Nobel Laureate Friedrich Hayek summarized the implications of the information problem confronted by central planners in the following manner:

> *If man is not to do more harm than good in his efforts to improve the social order, he will have to learn that in this, as in all other fields where essential complexity of an organized kind prevails, he cannot acquire the full knowledge which would make mastery of the events possible. He will therefore have to use what knowledge he can achieve, not to shape the results as the craftsman shapes his handiwork, but rather to cultivate growth by providing the appropriate environment, in the manner in which the gardener does this for his plants.*[20]

In other words, the economy is far too complex to be micromanaged. Instead, as stressed in Part 2, the best strategy for the achievement of growth and prosperity is the establishment of institutions and long-range policies that will create an environment in which individuals pursuing their own interest will undertake productive, wealth-creating activities.

Some years ago it was widely believed that government planning and "industrial policy" provided the keys to economic growth. Economists Paul Samuelson and Lester Thurow were among the leading proponents of this view, which dominated the popular media and intellectual circles during the 1970s and 1980s. They argued that market economies faced a dilemma: They would either have to move toward more government planning or suffer the consequences of slower growth and economic decline. The collapse of the Soviet system and the poor performance of the Japanese economy have largely eroded the popularity of this view. Nonetheless, many still believe that the government can direct various

20. Friedrich Hayek, "Pretence of Knowledge." Nobel Prize Lecture in Economics. Stockholm, Sweden. December 11, 1974.

sectors of the economy, such as health care and education. However, given the incentives and information problems accompanying central planning, this is unlikely to be the case.

More than two and a half centuries ago Adam Smith articulated the source of central-planning failures, including those that arise from efforts to plan specific sectors. (See the quote at the beginning of this element.) Unfortunately for government planners, individuals have minds of their own, what Smith calls "a principle of motion." When individuals face personal incentives that encourage them to act in ways that conflict with the central plan, problems arise. When governments move beyond the protective function and begin to subsidize various activities, operate enterprises, direct various sectors, and, in the extreme case, centrally plan the entire economy, invariably internal conflicts will arise and living standards will fall well below their potential.

The record of government planning in the United States illustrates this point. It is fraught with conflicts and internal inconsistencies:

- The federal government pays some farmers not to produce grain products, and at the same time, provides others with subsidized irrigation projects so they can grow more of the very same grain products.
- Government programs for dairy farmers keep the price of milk high, while government subsidizes the school lunch program to make the expensive milk more affordable.
- Federal regulations mandating stronger bumpers make automobiles safer, while the Corporate Average Fuel Economy (CAFE) standards make them lighter and less safe. Moreover, both regulations make automobiles more expensive.
- The federal government sends aid to poor countries with the stated aim of helping them develop, but then it imposes import restrictions that limit the ability of these countries to help

themselves (and Americans, too) by supplying United States consumers with quality products at attractive prices.

Economic analysis indicates that extensive use of government planning will lead to both economic inefficiency and cronyism. When government officials decide what is bought and sold, or the prices of those items, the first thing that will be bought and sold will be the votes of elected officials. When enterprises get more funds from governments and less from consumers, they will spend more time trying to influence politicians and less time trying to reduce costs and please customers. Predictably, the substitution of politics for markets will lead to economic regression and, in the words of Adam Smith, "the game will go on miserably, and the society must be at all times in the highest degree of disorder."

10. Competition is just as important in government as in markets.

Competition is a disciplinary force. In the marketplace, businesses must compete for the loyalty of customers. When firms serve their customers poorly, they generally lose business to rivals offering a better deal. Competition provides consumers with protection against high prices, shoddy merchandise, poor service, and/or rude behavior. Almost everyone recognizes this point with regard to the private sector. Unfortunately, the importance of competition in the public sector is often overlooked.

As discussed in the prior element, the structure of incentives confronted by government agencies and enterprises is not very conducive to efficient operation. There is nothing comparable to profits and losses to help one evaluate the performance of public sector agencies and enterprises. As a result, managers of government firms can often gloss over economic inefficiency. In the private sector, bankruptcy eventually weeds out inefficiency, but in the public sector there is no parallel mechanism for the termination of unsuccessful programs. There is little incentive to control spending. If an agency fails to spend this year's budget allocation, its case for a larger budget next year is weakened. Agencies typically go on a spending spree at the end of the budget period if appropriations have not yet been spent.

Given the structure of incentives within the public sector, it is vitally important that government enterprises face competition. If we are going to get the most from the available resources, private firms must be permitted to compete on a level playing field with government agencies and enterprises. For example, when governments operate vehicle maintenance departments, printing shops, food services, garbage collection services, street maintenance departments, schools, and similar agencies, private firms should be given an equal opportunity to compete with public enterprises. Competition can improve performance, reduce costs, and stimulate innovative behavior in government, as well as in the private sector.

Competition among decentralized government units—state and local governments—also can help protect citizens from government exploitation. A government cannot be oppressive when citizens can easily choose the "exit option"—move to another location that provides a level of government services and taxes more to their liking. Of course it is not as easy to walk away from your government as from your grocer! But the more government functions are decentralized, the easier it is for citizens to vote with their feet. Moreover, people can benefit from more competition between state and local government without moving themselves. The fact that some do move from less efficient to more efficient governments and that others could do the same motivates all state and local governments to become more sensitive to the concerns of their citizens.

Decentralization and variations in the activities of state and local governments can also enhance the ability of people to obtain government services more to their liking. Just as people differ regarding how much they want to spend on housing or automobiles, they will also have different views concerning expenditures on public services. Some will prefer higher levels of services and be willing to pay higher taxes for them. Others will prefer lower taxes and fewer government services. Some will want to fund government services with taxes, while others will prefer greater reliance on user charges. Within the framework of a decentralized political system, individuals will be able to group together with others desiring similar combinations of government services and taxes, and this grouping will make it possible for more people to obtain services more consistent with their preferences.

Moreover, the movement of people among the decentralized governmental units will also help improve efficiency. If a government levies high taxes (without providing a parallel quality of service) and regulates excessively, some individuals and businesses that make up their tax base will choose the exit option. Americans move a great deal, nearly 40 million each year. Moreover, their movements are not in a random pattern.

Between 2003 and 2013, the population of the nine states without a personal income tax grew by an average of 3.7 percent as the result of immigration from other states. During the same period, the nine states with the highest income taxes lost an average of 2 percent in population. Employment growth in the nine states without an income tax was more than double that of the high-tax states. Among the four most populous states, employment between 1990 and 2013 increased in the low-tax states of Texas and Florida by 65 percent and 46 percent respectively, compared to only 24 percent and 9 percent in the high-tax states of California and New York.[21] These movers are sending a message to high taxing, poorly

21. Stephen Moore, Arthur B. Laffer, and Joel Griffith, "1,000 People a Day: Why Red States Are Getting Richer and Blue States Poorer," Heritage Foundation (May 5, 2015).

run governments. Like businesses that realize losses when they fail to serve their customers, governments lose citizens when they serve them poorly.

Summarizing, decentralization allows people to move toward governmental units that provide desired public services at a low cost. In turn, the movements of voters will discipline governments and help keep them in line with the preferences of citizens.

However, if competition among decentralized governments is going to serve the interests of citizens, it must not be stifled by the policies of the federal government. When the national government subsidizes, mandates, and regulates the bundle of services provided by state and local governments, it undermines the competitive process among them. The best thing the central government can do is perform its limited functions well and remain neutral with regard to the operation and level of services of state, regional, and local governments.

Like private enterprises, units of government prefer protection from rivals. There will be a tendency for governments to seek a monopoly position. Therefore competition among governments will not evolve automatically. It will have to be incorporated into the political structure. This is precisely what the American founders were attempting to do when they designed the U.S. Constitution and the federal system of the United States.

Thinking About Constitutional Rules for Prosperity

There is enormous inertia—a tyranny of the status quo—in private and especially government arrangements. Only a crisis—actual or perceived—produces real change. When that crisis occurs, the actions that are taken depend on the ideas that are lying around. That, I believe, is our basic function: to develop alternatives to

existing policies, to keep them alive and available until the politi-
cally impossible becomes politically inevitable.[22]

—MILTON FRIEDMAN, 1976 NOBEL LAUREATE

What are the major messages of Part 3? First, economic analysis indicates that monopoly, public goods, and externalities are problems of the
market that encourage self-interested individuals to engage in counterproductive actions. These market failures create an opportunity for government intervention to enhance efficiency. But there is no assurance
this will be the case.

Political allocation, even when directed democratically, is merely an
alternative form of economic organization—and, like markets, it has shortcomings. There is government failure as well as market failure. Government failures include the following:

- Voters have little incentive to cast well-informed votes.
- When government moves beyond the protection of individual
  rights and becomes heavily involved in the allocation of scarce
  resources, elected political officials have a strong incentive
  to cater to the views of well-organized interest groups.
- Political favoritism will encourage wasteful rent-seeking.
- The political process tends to be shortsighted, which results
  in excessive use of debt and unfunded promises that are
  difficult, if not impossible, to keep.

If government is going to be a positive force for economic prosperity,
the rules of the political game must bring the self-interest of voters,

22. Friedman, Milton, *Capitalism and Freedom* (Chicago: University of Chicago Press,
2002).

politicians, and bureaucrats into harmony with economic progress. What would this look like and how might it be achieved?

Clearly, equal treatment under the law, federalism, and restraints on the powers of governments are central to the design of a political structure supportive of economic progress. Interestingly, economic analysis indicates that, to a large degree, the framers of the United States Constitution got the general structure right. They built checks and balances into the system. Legislation had to pass through two legislative bodies that, at the time, represented diverse and often conflicting interests, and the approval of the president is required for passage into law. Political power was divided among the legislative, executive, and judicial branches. The limitations on the powers of the central government provided for a decentralized federal system and still more dispersal of governmental powers. The permissible fiscal powers of the central government were enumerated (Article I, Section 8) and all other powers were allocated to the states and the people (Tenth Amendment). Congress was to levy uniform taxes in order "to provide for the common defence and general welfare." The clear intent was to prevent the use of the federal treasury as a tool to favor some groups and regions relative to others.

The Constitution also protected the property rights of individuals and their freedom to engage in voluntary exchange. The Fifth Amendment specified that private property shall not be "taken for public use without just compensation." States were prohibited from adopting legislation "impairing the obligation of contracts" (Article I, Section 10). Perhaps most importantly, states were prohibited from the erection of trade barriers, and as a result, the United States of America became the world's largest free-trade zone.

The United States Constitution sought to limit the ability of government, particularly the federal government, to politicize the economy and restrict the rights of citizens. Put another way, the Constitution was designed to promote government action based on agreement rather than coercion. Why is this important? People will agree to an action only when each party gains. Thus, actions based on agreement, whether undertaken through markets or government, will be mutually advantageous and will therefore promote the general welfare rather than the interests of some parties at the expense of others.

With the passage of time, however, the constraints of the original Constitution have eroded. The federal government is now involved in almost everything and the results are highly visible: political favoritism, special-interest spending, large budget deficits, excessive regulation, political corruption, and increased influence over many aspects of our lives. The challenge before us is to restore the intent of the constitutional rules and to develop a few new ones that will promote government action based on agreement and bring the political process back into harmony with economic progress.

How can this be accomplished? What provisions would a constitution designed to promote economic prosperity and stability contain? Several proposals flow directly from our analysis. Within the American context, we believe that the constitutional reforms outlined below would improve the operation of government and promote economic progress.

Reforms for Prosperity

We are aware that many of the reforms suggested below: (1) reflect the views of the authors of this book; and (2) are unlikely to be adopted in the immediate future. But economic analysis tells us that the United States and several other democratic countries are on an unsustainable path. If change does not occur, a crisis will result and it may well create an environment more conducive for constructive change, as Milton Friedman pointed out at the beginning of this section. It is in this spirit that we put forth the following nine constitutional reforms.

a. Neither the federal government nor state and local governments shall use their regulatory powers to take private property, either partially or in its entirety, for public use without paying the owner the full market value of the claimed property.

Court decisions have eroded the protection of private property provided by the Fifth Amendment. In recent years, state and local governments have used regulations to take or control private property without compensation, even though the property owner had violated the rights of no one. Moreover, court decisions have permitted state and local governments to take property from one party and then transfer it to another. This is an action that clearly conflicts with the intent of the "public use" provision of the Fifth Amendment. Courts have generally allowed such takings of private property as long as a legislative body deemed that the action was "in the public interest," or that the taking did not deny the owner all uses of his or her property. These are open doors for the abuse of private property rights that must be closed, and the Fifth Amendment should be revised to close them.

b. The right of individuals to compete in a business or profession and/or buy and sell legally tradable goods and services at mutually acceptable terms shall not be infringed by Congress or any of the states.[23]

The freedom of individuals to compete in business and engage in voluntary exchange activities is a cornerstone of both economic freedom and progress. Price controls, business and occupational entry restraints, laws restricting the exchange of goods and services across state boundaries, and other government regulations that restrain trade should be

---

23. Points (b) and (c) are the points of Milton and Rose Friedman, *Free to Choose* (New York: Harcourt Brace Jovanovich, 1980). See particularly chapter 10.

prohibited. Occupational licensing, mostly imposed at the state level, is a major anticompetitive device that restricts work opportunities, including those of many of the least well-off members of society. When there is concern about protecting the public, certification provides a superior option. With certification, buyers are provided with the information to make sound choices without closing off the opportunity for others to prove that they are capable providers. Predictably, licensing will be used to restrain trade and provide existing suppliers with monopoly power. This artificial barrier to entry needs to be removed.

c. Congress shall not levy taxes or impose quotas on either imports or exports.

The United States Constitution already prohibits the imposition of these trade restraints on exports. This prohibition should also be extended to imports. The freedom to trade is a basic human right, just like freedom of speech and freedom of religion. There is no reason why Americans should not be permitted to buy from, and sell to, whoever will give them the best deal, even if the trading partner lives in another country.

d. Whenever one quarter of the Members of the House or Senate of the United States transmits to the President their written declaration of opposition to a proposed federal regulation, it shall require a majority vote of the House and Senate to adopt that regulation.

This proposal, known as the "Regulation Freedom Amendment," has already been introduced in Congress. Each year, the number of administrative rules imposed by federal agencies is far greater than the number of laws passed by Congress. For example, in 2013 Congress passed 72 new laws that were signed by the president, but federal agencies imposed 3,659 new rules during the same year. Thus, the number of administrative rules was approximately fifty times the number of Congressionally passed laws.

These rules are supposed to provide details and clarify the meaning of congressional legislation. However, they often go well beyond this boundary. Once an agency adopts a rule, it is extremely difficult for Congress to alter it. As a result, the unchecked rule-making powers of the agencies make it possible for agencies to create law. Under the Constitution, federal laws must be passed by both branches of Congress and signed by the president. The Regulation Freedom Amendment would curtail the law-making authority of unelected agency officials and return it to Congress. The process would be easy and transparent. If a significant minority of the House or Senate opposed a regulation, the Congress would then be required to vote it up or down by a simple majority vote. Moreover, when it is easier for Congress to overturn their edicts, agency officials will exercise their rule-making powers more judiciously.

e. A constraint on the total level of federal spending must be imposed and the budget process should begin with the establishment of this constraint.

The federal budget process does not have a total spending constraint. As a result, as we have seen, federal spending is well beyond the optimal level, favor-seeking interests groups enrich themselves at the expense of the disorganized taxpayer, and numerous counterproductive programs reduce our potential income. A constitutional budget constraint should be imposed. It should be placed on spending because total expenditure is the best indicator of the burden of government. Households, businesses, and even state and local governments confront budget constraints. So, too, should the federal government.

There are several ways this might be done. One would be to adopt a constitutional amendment limiting federal spending to 20 percent of GDP, approximately the average of the past 50 years. Another would be to adopt a constitutional requirement that the president include a total spending constraint in the annual budget proposal. The constraint would then be submitted to Congress, and a two-thirds approval of both House and Senate required to alter it. This would make a single person, the only one elected by voters in all states, primarily responsible for the total spending level.

Still another way to establish the spending constraint would be to integrate a form into the federal personal income tax that would allow the votes of those paying this tax to determine whether federal spending during the upcoming fiscal year should be reduced, remain the same, or expanded. This alternative would have the advantage of permitting those paying for the spending to determine its level. Again, this spending constraint could only be over-ridden by a two-thirds vote of both legislative branches and approval by the president.[24]

The federal budgetary process is broken. Steps need to be taken to force legislators to more fully confront the opportunity costs of government spending. A meaningful budget constraint is an important step in that direction.

f. A two-thirds approval of both Houses of Congress shall be required for all expenditure programs of the federal government. At least three-fifths approval of the legislative branches of state government shall be required for the approval of expenditures by state governments.

This provision is designed to strengthen federalism and correct the tendency of power and control to flow toward the central government.

---

24. The federal government levies payroll, excise, and corporate taxes as well as the personal income tax. But the payroll tax is directed toward only two programs: Social Security and Medicare. Moreover, the benefits promised to Social Security recipients are related to the federal payroll taxes received. The personal income tax provides the bulk of federal revenue and it is the driving force underlying subsidies, special-interest spending, and the politicization of the economy. These factors, along with the ease with which the voting procedure can be integrated with the collection of the tax, explain why it makes sense to limit the voting on the budget constraint to those paying federal personal income tax.

The supermajority requirements for approval at the federal and state levels will mean that broad agreement, not just a simple majority, will be required before a project can be undertaken at these levels. This will reduce the prevalence of counterproductive projects. If a project is really productive, there will always be a method of finance that will result in everyone gaining. Thus, the supermajority provisions need not eliminate projects that truly increase wealth. They will, however, make it more difficult for special interests to use government as a tool for plunder. They will also help direct the spending activities of governments to the local level where competition among governments provides a stronger incentive to serve the interests of all citizens.

g. *A two-thirds approval of both Houses of Congress shall be required for the federal government to run an annual budget deficit or raise the overall limit on the national debt.*

As both economic analysis and recent history indicate, political incentives are biased toward debt financing. The current limit on the federal debt level is not a serious restraint, because every time the public debt ceiling is approached, a simple majority of Congress raises the limit. A constitutional provision requiring two-thirds approval for budget deficits and a revision in the debt limit would help Congress control its spending and borrowing addictions.

h. *A two-thirds approval of both Houses of Congress shall be required for the federal government to impose a mandated expenditure on state governments or private business firms.*

If this provision is not included, Congress will use mandated expenditures to escape the prior spending and borrowing limitations.

i. The function of the Federal Reserve System is to maintain the value of the currency and establish a stable price level. If the price level either increases or decreases by more than 4 percent annually during two consecutive years, all Governors of the Federal Reserve System shall be required to submit their resignations.

This provision would make it clear what the Federal Reserve System (Fed) is supposed to do. If the Fed establishes monetary stability, it is doing its part to promote economic stability and progress.

Final Thoughts

These provisions would enhance the protection of private ownership rights, promote competition, strengthen federalism, and help bring government spending and borrowing under control, while limiting the inclination of politicians to serve special-interest groups. They would be a positive step toward the restoration of government based on mutual agreement rather than the power to plunder. We have no doubt that they would assure growth and prosperity for future generations of Americans.

Parts 2 and 3 focused on national prosperity. The final section of this book will focus on personal prosperity by considering some practical choices you can make that will help you achieve a more prosperous life.

PART 4

*Twelve Key Elements
of Practical Personal Finance*

TWELVE KEY ELEMENTS OF
PRACTICAL PERSONAL FINANCE

1. Discover your comparative advantage.

2. Cultivate skills, attitudes, and entrepreneurship that increase productivity and make your services more valuable to others.

3. Use budgeting to help you spend your money effectively and save regularly.

4. Don't finance anything for longer than its useful life.

5. Two ways to get more out of your money: Avoid credit-card debt and consider purchasing used items.

6. Begin paying into a "rainy day" savings account every month.

7. Put the power of compound interest to work for you.

8. Diversify—don't put all of your eggs in one basket.

9. Indexed equity mutual funds can help you beat the experts without taking excessive risk.

10. Invest in stocks for long-run objectives, but as the need for money approaches, increase the proportion of bonds.

11. Take steps that will reduce risk when making housing, education, and other investment decisions.

12. Use insurance to help manage risk.

Introduction

Compared to Americans a couple of generations ago and their contemporaries worldwide, today's Americans have incredibly high income levels. Yet many are under financial stress. How can this be? The answer is that financial insecurity is mainly the result of the choices we make, not the incomes we earn.

If you do not take charge of your finances, they will take charge of you. As Yogi Berra, the great American philosopher (and late baseball star) said, "You've got to be very careful if you don't know where you are going, because you might not get there." In other words, each of us needs a plan. If we don't have one, we may end up where we do not want to be. The twelve elements in this part form the core of a practical plan. They focus on practical suggestions—things that you can do immediately—that will help you make better financial decisions whatever your current age, income level, or background.

Often, personal finance and investment decisions seem totally divorced from the world of economics. But they are not. As illustrated in Element 1, the principle of comparative advantage, which explains why countries benefit from specializing in the activities they do best, also explains why you as an individual can benefit from specialization in things you do well that are valued highly by others. Similarly, when it comes to building wealth over time, entrepreneurship, financial accountability, career planning, and investment in capital (especially human capital) are as valuable for individuals as they are for countries.

The principles, guidelines, and tools presented here could be divided into four categories: Elements 1 and 2 focus on how you can earn more; Elements 3 through 6 on how to get more value from your income; Elements 7 through 10 on earning more from your investments; and Elements 11 and 12 on management of risk.

The advice outlined here is basic, practical, and understandable. It will not make you a Wall Street wizard or an instant millionaire, but it will help you avoid major financial errors. More sophisticated plans are available. However, the search for perfection is often the enemy of positive action. Individuals who think they don't have the time or the expertise to develop a sound financial plan may fail even to apply simple guidelines that will help them avoid major financial troubles. This section will provide such guidelines.

Life is about choices. Our goal is to enhance your ability to choose options that will lead to a more successful life. John Morton, an associate of ours and one of the nation's leading economic educators, states:

> *I always told my students that life is not a lottery and life is not a zero-sum game. Your success will not take away from anyone else's success. Your success depends on your choices, and choices have consequences.*[1]

---

1. This quotation was provided in correspondence with the authors. John Morton was a legendary economics instructor at Homewood-Flossmoor High School in the Chicago area. He was also the founder and president of the Arizona Council on Economic Education and vice president for program development for the Council for Economic Education. Literally, tens of thousands of students have used his *Advanced Placement Economics* book in their preparation for the AP exams in economics.

Before examining how you can make better financial choices and get more from the resources available to you, we want to share a couple of thoughts about the importance of money and wealth. There is more to a good life than making money. When it comes to happiness, nonfinancial assets such as a good marriage, family, friends, fulfilling work, religious convictions, and enjoyable hobbies are far more important than money.[2] Thus the single-minded pursuit of money and wealth makes no sense.

At the same time, however, there is nothing unseemly about the desire for more wealth. This desire is not limited to those who are only interested in their personal welfare, narrowly defined. For example, the late Mother Teresa would have liked more wealth so that she could have done more to help the poor. Many people would like more wealth so they can donate more to religious, cultural, and charitable organizations, or do more to help elderly parents. No matter what our objectives in life, they are easier to achieve if we have less debt and more wealth. Thus all of us have an incentive to improve our financial decision-making. This section will offer twelve guidelines to help us do so.

1. Discover your comparative advantage.

The principle of comparative advantage is used most often to explain why international trade makes it possible for people in different countries to achieve higher living standards. As illustrated in Element 4 of Part 1, specialization according to the law of comparative advantage makes it possible for trading partners to produce more and achieve a higher income level. The principle of comparative advantage is just as important when individuals are considering occupational and business opportunities.

2. Arthur Brooks, president of the American Enterprise Institute, is one of the leading scholars on the determinants of happiness. For an overview of his views, see "A Formula for Happiness," *New York Times,* December 14, 2013, at: nytimes.com/2013/12/15 /opinion/sunday/a-formula-for-happiness.html?pagewanted=all&_r=0.

Like nations, individuals will be able to achieve higher income levels when they specialize, that is, concentrate their efforts on those things where they have a comparative advantage. Think about the relationship between your skills and opportunity costs. To pick one extreme, suppose that you are better than everyone else in every productive activity. Would that mean that you should try to spend some time on each activity? Or to go to another extreme, someone could be worse than everyone else. Would that individual be unable to gain from specialization because he or she would be unable to compete successfully in anything? The answer to both questions is no.

No matter how talented you are, you will be relatively more productive in some areas than others when opportunity costs are taken into account. Similarly, no matter how poor your ability to produce, you will be able to produce some things at a lower cost than others. You will be able to compete successfully in some areas and can gain by specializing where you have a comparative advantage.

Your comparative advantage is determined by your relative abilities, not your absolute abilities. For example, Mark Zuckerberg, cofounder of Facebook, has the skills not only to be a highly successful innovator and business entrepreneur, but he also has what it takes to be an outstanding computer programmer. It took a lot of programming skills and creativity to jump-start the popularity of a social media network in his dorm room at Harvard. While Zuckerberg was a highly skilled programmer, nonetheless, his comparative advantage was in the development of the innovative, social media features of Facebook. Similarly, even though the computer programmers working at Facebook are probably less skilled than Zuckerburg, their comparative advantages still lie in programming.

Individuals will always be better off if they are really good at something that is highly valued by others. This explains why people like Zuckerberg can make incredible amounts of money. He has become the world's richest individual under the age of thirty-five.

Some people may feel that they are at a disadvantage when they trade with others who earn far more money. But remember that trade benefits both parties. Generally, the more accomplished and wealthy the people with whom you trade (working for someone involves trade), the better off you are because your service is typically worth more to them than to those who are less accomplished and wealthy. For example, if the authors were entertainment agents, we would rather work for Oprah Winfrey than for any other media star because we would almost surely make more money that way.

The worst thing you can do is convince yourself, or be convinced by others, that you are somehow a victim and therefore unable to achieve success through your own effort and initiative. Some people start out with fewer advantages than others, but even those who are less advantaged can do extremely well if they make the effort and apply themselves intelligently. You need to take charge of your career development and plan how you can best develop your talents and use market cooperation to achieve your goals. No one else cares more about your personal success than you do. Neither does anyone else know more about your interests, skills, and goals.

We usually perceive of costs as something that should be kept as low as possible. But remember, costs reflect the highest valued opportunity given up when we choose an option. Thus, when you have attractive alternatives, your choices will be costly. Should you take that job at Starbucks to have more money while you're a student? Or should you take an extra course so that you can complete your college degree more quickly? Both options are attractive. Furthermore, as you improve your skills and your opportunities become even more attractive, the choice among options will be more costly.

In contrast, your costs will be low when you have very few good choices. For example, a very effective way of reducing the cost of reading this book is to get thrown in jail with it so that reading it is the only opportunity you have other than staring at the walls. This is obviously a bad idea. It would reduce the cost of doing one thing (a very desirable thing in our opinion) by eliminating your opportunity to do many other attractive things. You make yourself better off by increasing your opportunities, not by reducing them.

Young people are encouraged to get a good education so they will have more attractive opportunities later in life. But this is the same as encouraging them to increase the costs of all the choices they make. A good education will generally increase your productivity, and the amount employers are willing to pay you. This will enhance your earnings, but it also means you will have to turn down some attractive offers.

Sound career decision-making involves more than figuring out those things that you do best. It is also vitally important to discover where your passions lie—those productive activities that provide you with the most fulfillment. If you enjoy what you do and believe it is important, you will be happy to do more of it and work to do it better. Thus, competency and passion for an activity tend to go together. Moreover, real wealth is measured in terms of personal fulfillment. For example, the authors of this book (all economists) have found it satisfying to find answers to economic questions and to express what we know in ways that can help others better understand the corners of the world that we have examined professionally. Even though the hours are sometimes long, we find most of those hours enjoyable. What we do is not for everyone. But for us, with our interests, the joys of what we do more than make up for the rough patches.

2. *Cultivate skills, attitudes, and entrepreneurship that increase productivity and make your services more valuable to others.*

In a market economy, financial success reflects one's ability to provide others with value. This is true for both employees and businesses. If you want to achieve high earnings, you had better figure out how to provide others with services they value highly.

As previously stressed, improved knowledge, higher skill level, and experience generally increase productivity and enhance one's ability to provide valuable services to others. As a result, investments in human capital—education, training, and other forms of skill acquisition—can improve both productivity and earnings. But other personal attributes also influence productivity. Two of the most important are personal attitudes and thinking entrepreneurially. The importance of these two attributes as a source of productivity is closely related to what psychologists call emotional intelligence (EQ). Many psychologists now believe that EQ is more important than IQ as a determinant of personal success.[3] Even economists often overlook these two vitally important sources of personal productivity. Let's consider each of them.

How does one's personal attitude impact productivity and success? Consider the following simple thought experiment. Suppose an employer is evaluating two potential employees. The first has the following set of attributes: honesty, dependability, persistence, reliability, trustworthiness, respect for others, desire to learn and improve, and ability to work with others. The second has a different set: disrespect for others, unreliable, quarrelsome, contempt for education, vulgarity of speech, blaming others for problems, dishonesty, and reliance on alcohol and drugs. If you were the employer, which would you hire? Predictably, most would hire the first candidate because those attitudes are success-oriented. Other things constant, employees with these positive attitudes are more productive. In contrast, the second set of attributes are failure-oriented. They will undermine productivity and the ability of the employee to work with others.

---

3. See "What Is Emotional Intelligence (EQ)?" by Michael Akers & Grover Porter at: psychcentral.com/lib/what-is-emotional-intelligence-eq/.

If you want to be successful, you need to cultivate, develop, and strengthen the first set of attributes. They need to become habits—the core values of your life. Equally important, you need to cast the second set out of your life. Do not let anyone, including friends, convince you that any of the failure attributes are "cool." They are the path to trouble, and you do not want to go down that route.

There is some good news here: You can choose the success attitudes rather than the failure ones. Moreover, you can do so regardless of your family background, current income, educational level, or choice of career. Your attitudes will exert a huge impact on your future financial success. Positive attitudes will help you overcome other disadvantages, such as a poor education or a financially restricted childhood.

Of course, if you choose the failure attitudes, you can blame others: your family, your neighborhood, the schools you attended, or society in general. These factors may influence your choices, but they do not determine them. Your attitude characteristics are under your control. If you grew up in a troublesome environment, it may be more difficult to attain and maintain these attitudes. But a person who overcomes a negative environment is admired and respected by almost all. A troublesome background can even help launch your success if you choose to develop positive attitudes.

Some of you may be thinking, "My attitudes are my own business. No one is going to tell me what to do or change my behavior." Suppose a business owner, let's call him Sam, has this perspective. Sam ignores the wishes of consumers and instead provides what he thinks consumers should value. Sam is free to make this choice. However, if he does so, he will pay a price in the form of losses and business failure. Similarly, potential employees are free to "do their own thing." They can ignore how their attitudes and behavior affect productivity and employability. But, like the business that ignores the desires of consumers, people who ignore how their attitudes and behavior influence their productivity will pay a price in the form of poor opportunities and low earnings. None of us is an island unto ourselves. If we want others to provide us with income, we need to cooperate and make our services valuable to them.

The bottom line is straightforward: Success-oriented attitudes are a highly important determinant of financial success. You cannot buy these attitudes. Neither can someone else provide them to you. You must choose them and integrate them into your life. Further, if you do so, it is a near certainty that you will have a substantial degree of economic success. But the opposite is also true: If your life is largely a reflection of the failure set of attributes, it is a virtual certainty that your future will be characterized by financial troubles and personal bitterness.

Entrepreneurial thinking is also a personal attribute that can enhance your productivity. While entrepreneurship is often associated with decision-making in business, in a very real sense all of us are entrepreneurs. We are constantly making decisions about the development and use of knowledge, skills, and other resources under our control. Our financial success will reflect the outcome of these choices.

If you want to be financially successful, think entrepreneurially. Put another way, focus on how to develop and use your talents and mobilize available resources to provide others with things that they value highly.

Providing others with goods and services that are highly valued compared to their cost is the key to financial success. Consider the hypothetical case of Robert Jones, a land developer. Jones purchases large land tracts, subdivides them, and adds various amenities such as roads, sewage disposal, golf courses, and parks. Jones will profit if he is able to sell the plots for more than the cost of the land, the various amenities he has constructed, and his labor services, including the earnings forgone in his best alternative pursuit. If his actions are profitable, they will increase the value of the resources and help others by providing them with better home sites than are available elsewhere. Jones's financial success or failure is dependent on his ability to enhance the value of resources.

Once you begin to think entrepreneurially—to think about how you can increase the value of your services to others, do not underestimate your ability to achieve success. Entrepreneurial talent is often found in unexpected places. Who would have thought that a middle-aged, milk-shake-machine salesman, Ray Kroc, would revolutionize the franchising business and expand a single McDonald's restaurant in San Bernardino, California, into the world's largest fast-food chain? Did anyone in the 1960s expect Sam Walton to take a couple of small stores in Arkansas (one of the nation's poorest states) and transform them into the largest retailer in America during the 1990s? How could anyone have anticipated that Ted Turner, the owner of an outdoor sign business in Atlanta, would develop one of the world's largest cable news networks, CNN?

These are high-profile cases, but the same pattern occurs over and over. Successful business and professional leaders often come from diverse backgrounds that appear to be largely unrelated to the areas of their achievement. But they have something in common: They are good at discovering better ways of doing things and strategically acting on opportunities to increase the value of resources that have been overlooked by others.

Self-employed entrepreneurs are disproportionately represented among the wealthy. While the self-employed constitute about one-sixth of the labor force, they account for two-thirds of America's millionaires. Four major factors contribute to the financial success of self-employed entrepreneurs. First, they are good at identifying and acting on attractive opportunities that have been overlooked by others. Second, they are willing to take risk. Greater risk and higher returns go together. To a degree, the higher incomes of self-employed entrepreneurs are merely compensation for the uncertainties accompanying their business activities. Third, they have a high investment rate. Self-employed business owners often channel a large share of their income into the growth and expansion of their business. Fourth, they generally love what they do and therefore work long hours.

Employees, too, can adopt the characteristics that contribute to the high-income status and wealth of self-employed entrepreneurs. They can invest their savings in stocks and thereby achieve the above-average returns that come with the risk of business ownership. If they desire, they can also generate more income and accumulate more wealth through higher rates of investment and more hours of work.

Perhaps most important, employees can gain by "thinking like entrepreneurs." Just as the incomes of business entrepreneurs depend on their ability to satisfy customers, the earnings of employees depend on their ability to make themselves valuable to employers, both current and prospective. If employees want to achieve high earnings, they need to develop skills, knowledge, attitudes, and work habits that are highly valued by others.

The entrepreneurial way of thinking is also crucially important when making decisions about education. Education will not enhance your earnings very much unless you acquire knowledge and develop skills that make your services more valuable to others. These include the ability to write well, communicate with clarity, use basic math tools, collect and interpret data and information, as well as specific skills that can set you apart from the crowd and raise your productivity. Developing skills that make you more valuable to others is vitally important both in and outside of the brick-and-mortar institutions of secondary and postsecondary education. Today, having a bachelor's degree is no longer guaranteed to catch an employer's eye and result in a ticket to a high-paying job. Employment and educational markets change rapidly. The best way to find a job is to think entrepreneurially and discover ways to serve others through formal education and showcasing your job readiness. Massive open online courses, certificate programs, and internships can be helpful in this area.

Development and use of your talents in ways that provide large benefits to others is a key to financial success. It is also central to what Arthur Brooks calls "earned success." Moreover, earned success is the central element of happiness and life satisfaction. No one can give you earned success; you must achieve it. Earned success is present when your education, work, and lifestyle choices reflect the purpose of your life. Throughout our careers, we have asked our students what they want to do with their lives. In one form or another, the response is nearly always the same: I want to do things that will make the world a better place to live. Of course, individuals will differ with regard to how they plan to do so. But, regardless of their plans, a positive set of attitudes and an entrepreneurial thought process will enhance their ability to live a meaningful, fulfilling, and happy life.

3. Use budgeting to help you spend your money effectively and save regularly.

> *Money is only a tool. It will take you wherever you wish, but it will not replace you as the driver.*[4]
>
> —AYN RAND

Most financial insecurity today is the product of unsound choices. Spending more than you earn, building up debt without concern for how to repay it, lack of budgeting, and other unwise financial habits create havoc and cause stress. A commitment to budgeting is key to obtaining a healthy financial life, building wealth, and achieving your personal goals. People, like nations, build wealth through saving and investment. But successful building of wealth also takes strategic planning. There

4. Ayn Rand, *Atlas Shrugged* (New York: Random House, 1957): 411.

must be a plan in place to guide how the spending, saving, and investment are directed toward wealth creation. For the individual or household, that plan is a **budget**. A budget helps you channel your funds toward sound spending, regular saving, and diversified investments in a manner that will provide you with the most value from your income.

Effective budgeting is an ongoing process, not a one-time event. It is comprised of two specific actions. First, you must create the initial budget that is simply a document that identifies all of your planned or expected spending for a period of time. Most people create a monthly budget but a yearly budget is also common. It is important to carefully consider all of your spending, not just the highly visible spending like groceries, car payments, and rent or mortgage. Don't forget about birthday gifts, license tag renewal fees, magazine subscriptions, and oil changes for your car. Estimate your monthly or annual income; then identify where you are going to spend every penny. We recommend zero-based budgeting, which means that saving and investment are specific items in your budget, not just the leftover balance (if there is any).

The second action is documentation of actual spending and making needed budget adjustments. Keeping track of all spending and placing it into the categories of your budget provides valuable information about your habits and the progress made toward achievement of your financial goals. Tracking your spending will also help you develop a better, more precise budget in the future. For example, if you fail to include a spending item or two in your initial budget, when that actual spending is observed, you can then make sure to include it in your new budget next time. Suppose you budget $100 for restaurant meals for the month but then realize that you actually spent $150. You will know to either change your budget or your spending to account for this difference. The documentation of your actual spending provides you with a feedback mechanism that will help you make adjustments to your budget and spending in the future.

Budgeting your income and monitoring your behavior will help you evaluate your spending and direct it toward the categories that will provide you with the most overall value. Four simple steps will get you on the path to financial stability: Begin immediately, set goals, get tools, and design a budget to meet your goals.

Step 1. Start now and increase the likelihood of success! Don't fool yourself into thinking that budgeting is only for people with jobs, or high salaries, or that you'll start "later." Children receiving allowance, students receiving support from their parents, and people without direct incomes should still budget and develop goals. Budgeting will not be easier when you are older or when you are earning more money. In fact, it will probably be more complex. It is easy to procrastinate. People who budget, spend their money wisely, and save for the future generally started early when their incomes were relatively low.[5]

Step 2. Set goals. Incentives matter. Recognize this in your personal life, and let your goals drive your actions. Set short-, medium-, and long-term financial goals and incorporate them into your budget. Short-term milestones can be achieved within the next year and provide immediate gratification. Depending on your situation, they might include the elimination of the credit-card debt on your highest interest rate loan, a significant increase in your rainy day savings account for coverage of unexpected expenditures, or money for an upgrade of your phone or other technological device. Mid-term goals are achieved over a longer period—anywhere between one and three years. Purchasing a pre-owned

---

5. Thomas Stanley and William D. Danko point out in their bestseller, *The Millionaire Next Door* (Atlanta: Longstreet Press, 1996), that the most common characteristic of millionaires is that they have lived beneath their means for a long time. Over half of them never received any inheritance and fewer than 20 percent received 10 percent or more of their wealth from inheritance (p. 16).

car with cash, putting 20 percent down on a home or condo, and building a solid savings account leading to a well-diversified portfolio are examples of goals that will generally require more time to achieve. Finally, saving and investing for your children's college and for retirement, and paying off student loans or a home **mortgage** provide examples of longer-term goals that many will want to pursue.

As indicated earlier, saving and investing should be a specific category in your budget. Obviously the sooner you start saving and spending strategically, the more wealth you will build. What is not so obvious is how much more wealth you can accumulate by starting early. Even the smallest amount saved or invested today can make a very big difference. Consider the following long-range plan.

Start regularly saving $2 a day for two years when you turn twenty-two years of age. That's probably not as much as you will spend on coffee, bottled water, snacks or have in loose change at the end of the day. Then from your twenty-fourth until your twenty-sixth birthday, begin saving $3 a day. That's just a dollar more and your income will probably have increased. Between the ages of twenty-six and thirty, bump up your savings amount to $4 per day. By not spending this amount daily and putting it aside in an account with a positive rate of return, you won't cramp your style much. By the time you reach thirty, you will have saved $9,490, plus the interest received—quite a nice sum. Saving $2, $3, or $4 a day really adds up.

But here's the real surprise. By the time you retire at age sixty-seven, the saving from just this early nine-year period can add more than $150,000 to your wealth if invested wisely, and that's in today's purchasing power. This will be the case if you earn a rate of return equal to about what the stock market has yielded over the last eight decades (more on this rate of return and the power of compound interest in future elements). Moreover, if you start early, you are far more likely to continue with a regular savings plan throughout your life.

Step 3. Get tools to assist with your budgeting. Don't re-create the wheel by starting with a blank piece of paper to develop a budget. With today's websites, spreadsheets, and apps, budgeting has never been easier. A plethora of resources exist at little or no money cost. Literally, they are available at your fingertips. Conduct an Internet search for "budgeting tools," and find numerous high-quality and secure budgeting options. Choose one that helps you become meticulous in logging your expenses and income, keeps your financial goals in front of you, issues payment reminders, helps you control any impulses to spend outside your budget, and links you to options on how to achieve those goals. Make a habit of using your selected budgeting tool. Keeping track of your spending and income can be easy with the right tools. For more on budgeting basics and suggestions for creative consumption and savings plans, visit CommonSenseEconomics.com/supplementals.

Step 4. Devise a plan of action: Create a personal budget with actual and proposed items to achieve your goals. Although we constantly think about all the things we "need" to buy, there are very few things most of us are required to have beyond adequate food, clean water, basic shelter, and simple clothes. The best way to see where you can begin to achieve your goals is by listing your "needs" and separating them from your "wants." Reduce your wants to make way for savings and investing, and for devising a plan within your budget to meet your short-, medium-, and long-term goals. This places you in the driver's seat of your financial life.

An architect does not build a house without a blueprint. A surgeon does not effectively remove a patient's appendix without coordinating her plans with the other members of the medical team. An athlete does not end up competing at the Olympics without committing to a philosophy of success long before reaching the Olympics. Developing a detailed plan of action, sticking to it, and updating it when necessary are essential if you are going to succeed in all aspects of life, including your financial life.

Each budgetary item needs to be evaluated within the context of the others. Since you have limited income, increased spending in one area translates into decreased spending in another, unless new sources of income are identified. As stressed in Part 1, every choice has an opportunity cost. Consider yours when making a spending decision. Examine the big picture through your budgetary lens. Figure out your monthly basics— show how much you earn, pay in taxes, save, invest, spend, and face in debt.

Regardless of your occupation, income, or position in life, the two actions in the budgeting process—creation of your budget and tracking and adjusting your spending to improve your welfare—will help you systematically examine and guide your spending to get where you want to go. Make your plan crystal clear and become the CEO of you. Commit to creating a budget that organizes your spending, controls your debt, provides emergency funds, helps you meet various financial goals, and supplies funds for investing.

The next time you are thinking about all the things you "need," recognize that you do not really have to have many of them. Remember that spending today costs you in terms of your future wealth. We aren't suggesting that you live a life of deprivation so you can be rich in the future. That makes no sense. But there are many creative ways to reduce spending and increase saving. Budgeting and laying out a savings plan will produce immediate satisfaction, help you gain a sense of financial control and security, and build wealth for the future.

Dave Ramsey, one of the nation's leading financial advisors, highlights the importance of making a personal commitment to forming sound money habits. He claims: "The thing I have discovered about working with personal finance is that the good news is that it is not rocket science. Personal finance is about 80 percent behavior. It is only about

20 percent head knowledge."[6] After reading the entirety of Part 4, you will have the head knowledge. Are you ready to focus and commit to aligning your consumption, saving, borrowing, and earning decisions with those that promise financial stability and lead to a rewarding life?

Elements 4 through 12 will provide additional details on how to get more out of your spending, avoid imprudent debt, plan for unexpected expenditures, earn an attractive return on your investments, and minimize your vulnerability to the risks of life.

4. Don't finance anything for longer than its useful life.

What happens when you borrow money to purchase vacations, clothing, or other goods that are quickly consumed or that depreciate in value? What happens when you take out a forty-eight-month loan in order to purchase a used automobile that will be worn out in two years? The answer to both questions is the same: You will soon be making payments on things that have little or no value to you or anyone else. These payments will lead to frustration, bitterness, and financial insecurity.

Financing an item over a time period lengthier than the useful life of the asset forces you to pay in the future for something that will no longer be of value to you. As a result, you will be forced to reduce your future consumption. Further, this strategy increases your indebtedness and you will become poorer in the future. It is a path to financial disaster.

Does it ever make sense for an individual or family to purchase a good on credit? The answer is "yes," but only if the good is a long-lasting asset and if the borrowed funds are repaid before the asset is worn out. This way you pay for a good as you use it.

Very few purchases meet these criteria. Three categories of major

6. See "The Truth About Debt Management." Dave Ramsey. N.p., October 25, 2014. www.daveramsey.com/mobile/truth-about-detail/storyID/the-truth-about-debt -management/.

expenditures come to mind: housing, automobiles, and education. If maintained properly, a new house may provide useful life for forty or fifty years into the future. Under these circumstances the use of a thirty-year mortgage to finance the expenditure is perfectly sensible. Similarly, if an automobile can reasonably be expected to be driven five or six years, there's nothing wrong with financing it over a time period of forty-eight months or less. When long-lasting assets are still generating additional income or a valuable service after the loans used to finance their purchase are repaid, some of the loan payments are actually a form of savings and investment, which will enhance the net worth of a household. Like housing, investments in education generally provide net benefits over a lengthy time period. Young people investing in a college education through debt financing may reap dividends in the form of higher earnings. The educational investment will be a good one if, over the next twenty or thirty years, the higher earnings are sufficient to pay off the borrowed funds. But there are risks here: If the additional education does not increase your future earnings, at least not by much, it may be exceedingly difficult to repay the borrowed funds. (Note: This issue will be considered in more detail in Part 4, Element 11.)

For most households the implications of this guideline are straightforward: Do not borrow funds to finance anything other than housing, automobiles, and education. Furthermore, make sure that funds borrowed for the purchase of these items will be repaid well before the expiration of the asset's useful life. Application of this simple guideline will go a long way toward keeping you out of financial trouble.

5. *Two ways to get more out of your money: Avoid credit-card debt and consider purchasing used items.*

Most of us would like to have more in the future without having to give up much today. Many, including those with incomes well above average, do two things that undermine this objective. First, they go into debt to buy things before they can afford them. Second, they insist on buying new items even when used ones would be just as serviceable and far more economical.

Imprudent use of credit cards can be a huge stumbling block to financial success. Although many people are careful with cards, others act as if an unused balance on a credit card is like money in the bank. This is blatantly false and dangerous thinking. An unused balance on your credit card merely means that you have some additional borrowing power; it does not enhance your wealth or provide you with more money. It is best to think of your credit card as a means of using what you have in your checking account. If you have funds in your checking account, you can use your credit card to access those funds—if you pay off the bill every month. If you don't have sufficient funds in your account, don't make the purchase.

While credit cards and their electronic counterparts (such as PayPal and ApplePay) are convenient to use, they are also both seductive and a costly method of borrowing. Because credit cards make it easy to run up debt, they are potentially dangerous. Some people seem unable to control the impulse to spend when there is an unused balance on their cards.[7] If you have this problem you need to take immediate action! You need to get your hands on a pair of scissors and cut up all of your credit cards. If you do not, they will lead to financial misfortune.

Making purchases on your credit card makes it look as though you are buying more with your money, but the bill invariably comes at the end of the month. This presents another temptation: the option to send

---

7. Some may need creative methods of controlling impulse purchases with a credit card. If this is the case, economist and financial advisor William C. Wood suggests that you freeze your credit card inside a block of ice in your refrigerator. By the time the ice thaws, your impulse to buy may have cooled. For an excellent book on personal finance written from a Christian perspective, see William C. Wood, *Getting a Grip on Your Money* (Downers Grove, Illinois: Inter-Varsity Press, 2002).

in a small payment to cover the interest and a tiny percentage of the balance and keep most of your money to spend on more things. If you choose this option and continue to run up your balance, however, you will quickly confront a major problem—the high interest rates being charged on the unpaid balance.

It is common for people to pay interest charges of 15 to 18 percent on their credit-card debt. This is far higher than most people, even successful investors, can earn on their savings and investments. As we shall see in later elements, you can become wealthy earning 7 percent per year on your investments. Unfortunately, high interest rates on outstanding debt will have the opposite impact. Paying 15 to 18 percent on your credit-card debt can drive even a person with a good income into poverty.

Consider the example of Sean, a young professional who decides to take a few days relaxing in the Bahamas. The trip costs Sean $1,500, which he puts on his credit card. But instead of paying the full amount at the end of the month, Sean pays only the minimum, and he keeps doing so for the next ten years, when the bill is finally paid off. How much did Sean pay for his trip, assuming an 18 percent interest rate on his credit card? He pays $26.63 per month for 120 months, or a total of $3,195.40. So Sean pays his credit-card company more than he paid for the air travel, hotel, food, and entertainment.

Sean could have taken the trip for a whole lot less by planning ahead and starting to make payments to himself before the trip, instead of making payments to the credit-card company after the trip. By saving $75 a month at 5 percent per year in compound interest (we will discuss compound interest in Element 7) for twenty months, Sean could have had $1,560.89 for the trip, and not the $3,195.40 he ended up paying (including interest) for the same trip (but taken earlier) on the credit card. In other words, by saving and planning to make his trip, instead of running up credit-card debt to pay for it, Sean could take two trips for less than what he ended up paying for one on credit.

In some cases, you may already have a sizable credit-card bill. It would have been better if you had avoided that debt, but it does provide an opportunity for you to get a very high return: Every dollar you save to pay down a credit-card debt effectively earns an interest rate of 18 percent, or whatever you are paying on the debt.

Look at it this way. If you put a dollar in an investment that is paying 18 percent, then one year from now it has added $1.18 to your net worth. If you save a dollar to pay off your credit-card debt, then one year from now it has also added $1.18 to your net worth. Your debt will be that much lower—first, from the dollar you saved that reduced your debt initially and, second, from the 18 cents you would have otherwise owed in interest.

Even if your credit-card rate is less than 18 percent, it is still much higher than what you will consistently earn on any other savings program you will ever have, unless you are extraordinarily lucky or a spectacular investor. Of course you may not feel as though your savings are really earning 18 percent, since the money isn't actually being paid into your investment accounts. But it amounts to the same thing. The very first thing anyone who has a credit-card debt and is serious about achieving financial success should do is *pay that debt off*, from savings if necessary.

What if you do not have the funds to pay off your credit-card bill? Then take out a bank loan—the interest rate will be lower than your credit-card rate—and, based on the budgeting principles presented in Element 3, develop a plan to pay off the loan as quickly as possible. Of course, you also need to make sure that you do not run up any other credit-card debt.

In addition to avoiding credit-card debt or paying it off immediately, you can stretch your money by buying used items when they will serve you almost as well as new ones. The problem with buying things new is that they depreciate or decline in value almost immediately. Thus, while new items can be purchased, they cannot be owned as new items for long. Almost as soon as an item is purchased, it becomes "used" in terms of market value.

Buying things that are used—or, in today's parlance, pre-owned—can reap substantial savings. Consider the cost of purchasing a new automobile compared with a used one. For example, if you buy a brand-new Toyota Camry, which will cost you about $28,000, and trade it in after one year, you will receive about $18,000, or $10,000 less than you paid for it. If you drove the car fifteen thousand miles, then your depreciation cost—the cost to you of the decline in the car's value—is 66 cents per mile.

But instead of buying a new Camry, you can buy one that is a year old from a dealer. You will pay about $20,000. This is $8,000 less than it cost new (and about $2,000 more than the original owner received from the dealer).

Given how long cars last if you take care of them, you should easily be able to get excellent service from your used Camry for eight years, at which time you can probably sell it for about $2,000. Assuming that you drove 15,000 miles per year, your depreciation cost per mile will be $18,000/120,000 miles, or just 15 cents. This is 51 cents per mile less than the cost of driving a new car every year. Staying with the assumption that you drive 15,000 miles a year, the depreciation saving from the used car is $7,650 every year. Of course your repair bills may be somewhat higher after the car is a few years old, but even if they average $1,650 a year (very doubtful), you will still save $6,000 each year by sacrificing that new car smell.

Many other items are just as functional used as new and often much less expensive. Clothes, furniture, appliances, refurbished phones, and toys come immediately to mind. You may want to spend some time at garage sales or secondhand stores. Given the value of your time, however, there are other ways to find used items. Craigslist, eBay, and apps provide alternatives that reduce time spent and transaction costs. In a few "touches," you can find items that are both in excellent condition and priced significantly below retail. Of course, there are some cases when buying new is economical. We are merely encouraging you to consider the potential savings that can often be derived from used purchases without giving up much in terms of consumer satisfaction. Look for opportunities to get more value from your money.

6. Begin paying into a "rainy day" savings account every month.

We have talked about the value of saving for your future. But you also need a rainy day savings account. What is that? Life has an endless string of surprise occurrences: the car breaks down, the roof leaks, you have a plumbing problem, your child breaks an arm—just to name a few.[8] We can't predict which ones will occur, or when. But we can predict that over any long period of time, each household will confront such costly items. Thus, it makes sense to plan for them. This is what your rainy day savings account is for. It will help you deal with unexpected bills that could otherwise put you under severe emotional stress and into a financial bind.

The alternative is to wait until the surprise events occur and then try to devise a plan to deal with them. This will generally mean running up credit-card balances or some other method of borrowing funds on highly unfavorable terms. Then you have to figure out how you're going to cover the interest charges and eventually repay the funds. All of this leads to anxiety that is likely to result in unwise financial decisions.

How much should you set aside regularly to deal with such events? One approach would be to make a list of the various surprises of the past year and estimate how much each one cost you. Think about car repairs, unexpected travel, doctor's visits, a home appliance replaced—anything that you didn't expect to happen last year. Add the costs up, divide that

8. Professor William C. Wood calls such items "SIT expenditures." Wood indicates that "SIT stands for two things: (1) sit down when you get an unexpected bill; and (2) surprises, insurance and taxes."

number by twelve, and begin channeling that amount monthly into your rainy day savings account.

You might even want to pay a little more into the account just in case you confront higher future spending in this area. After all, if you pay too much into the account, you can build up a little cushion. If the funds in the account continue to grow, eventually you can use some of them for other purposes or allocate them into your retirement savings program. The key point is to consider the monthly allocations into your rainy day savings account as a mandatory rather than an optional budget item. Thus they should be treated just like your mortgage payment, electric bill, and other regular expenditures.

A rainy day savings account allows you to purchase a little peace of mind rather than worrying about the financial bumps of life. With such an account, you will be able to deal confidently with expenditures that, while unpredictable as to timing, can nonetheless be anticipated with a fair degree of accuracy. During periods when your surprise expenditures are below average, the balance in your rainy day savings account will grow. When the surprise expenditures are atypically large, the funds in your account will be drawn down, but you can remain calm because you are prepared. This is an important element of what it means for you to "take charge of your money" rather than allowing "money to take charge of you."

7. *Put the power of compound interest to work for you.*

Compound interest is the most powerful force in the universe.[9]

—ALBERT EINSTEIN

9. Mignon McLaughlin. N.d. BrainyQuote.com. Retrieved October 24, 2015, from BrainyQuote.com website: www.brainyquote.com/quotes/quotes/m/mignonmcla158995 .html. There is some controversy about whether this statement was made by Albert Einstein but he clearly made similar statements highlighting the power of compound interest.

In Element 3 we emphasized the importance of budgeting regularly, saving habitually and spending your money effectively. There are two major reasons for starting earlier rather than later. First, as discussed, those who yield now to the many excuses not to start budgeting, saving, and spending wisely will have a hard time doing so later. But in this element we want to talk more about the second reason to begin saving right away: the big payoff that comes from starting early.

A small head start in your savings program leads to a substantial increase in the payoff. Recall the example in Element 3 of the additional retirement wealth a young person could have by saving a modest amount from age twenty-two to thirty. Giving up just a little less than $9,500 in purchasing power for those nine years can easily add over $150,000 to retirement wealth at age sixty-seven. The key to converting a small amount of money now into a large amount later is to start saving immediately to take full advantage of the "miracle of compound interest."

Compound interest is not really a miracle, but sometimes it seems that way. Despite the fact that it is easy to explain how compound interest works, the results are truly amazing. Compound interest is simply earning interest on interest. If you don't spend the interest earned on your savings this year, the interest will add to both your savings and the interest earned next year. By doing the same thing each year in the future, you then earn interest on your interest on your interest, etc. This may not seem like much, and for the first few years it doesn't add that much to your wealth. But before too long your wealth begins growing noticeably, and the larger it becomes the faster it grows. It's like a small snowball rolling down a snow-covered mountain. At first it increases in size slowly. But each little bit of extra snow adds to the size, which allows even more snow to be accumulated, and soon it is huge, growing rapidly, and coming right at you.

The importance of starting your savings program early is explained by how compound interest sets the stage for its accelerating effect later.

The savings you make right before retirement won't add much more to your retirement wealth than the amount you save—a little but not much. The snowball that starts near the bottom of the mountain won't be much bigger when it stops rolling. So the sooner you start saving, the more time that early savings will have to grow, and the more dramatic the growth will be.

Consider a simple example. Assume a sixteen-year-old is deciding whether or not to start smoking. This is an important choice for several reasons, health considerations being the most important. However, in addition to the health factor, there is a financial reason for not smoking. The average price of cigarettes in the United States is approximately $7.50 a pack. So if our teenager—let's call him Roger—decides against smoking, he will save $2,737.50 a year (assuming he would have smoked a pack a day). Suppose that instead of spending this amount on something else, Roger invests it in a mutual fund that provides an annual rate of return of 7 percent in real terms—that is, after adjusting for inflation. (Note: This 7 percent return is approximately equal to the annual rate of return of the **Standard & Poor's (S&P) 500 Index,** an index of the five hundred largest U.S. firms that mirrors the performance of the overall stock market.) As Exhibit 13 illustrates, if Roger keeps this up for ten years, when he is twenty-six he will have accumulated $37,823 from savings of $27,375. Not bad for a rather small sacrifice—one that is, in fact, good for Roger.

But this is just liftoff; the payoff from compound interest is merely getting started. If Roger keeps this savings plan going until he is thirty-six, he will have $112,225 from savings of $54,750. Continuing until he is forty-six will find him with $258,586 from savings of $82,125. And now the afterburners really start kicking in. By the time Roger is fifty-six he will have $546,501 from saving contributions of $109,500. As Exhibit 13 shows, when he retires at age sixty-seven he will have $1,193,512 from direct contributions of only $139,613. Thus, by choosing not to smoke

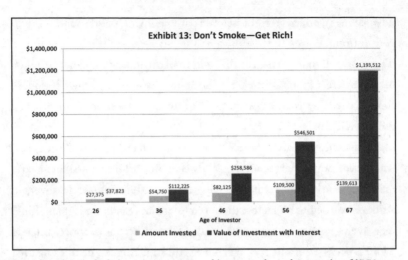

Source: Authors' calculations. Assumes not smoking one pack per day at a price of $7.50 per pack, and earning interest of 7 percent per year.

and investing the funds, Roger accumulates nearly $1.2 million in retirement benefits—and this figure is in dollars with today's purchasing power![10]

Alternatively, consider what would happen if Roger smoked from age sixteen to twenty-six, then stopped smoking and started saving the price of a pack of cigarettes every day. It is good that he stopped smoking, and he will still benefit from the savings. But by postponing his savings program by ten years, instead of having $1,193,512 at age sixty-seven, Roger will have only $587,494. Delaying a fifty-one-year saving program by ten years costs Roger $606,018 at retirement!

You don't have to completely give up something in order to achieve substantial savings. Making small sacrifices in consumption can yield

10. Our calculations assume that your investments yield a return of 7 percent every year. Obviously this is unlikely to happen. Even though you can expect an average annual return of approximately 7 percent, this return will vary from year to year. This can make a difference in how much you accumulate at retirement, but the difference is likely to be small.

equally powerful results. Instead of buying the premium cup of coffee every morning, purchase the generic one or make the cup at home. Instead of eating lunch at a restaurant every day, bring your lunch one or two days a week. Skip the soft drink or beverage at a restaurant and drink water. Carpool or take the bus to work once a week to save gas money. Roger gave up smoking to save $52.50 per week and invested it instead. You, too, can make changes in your consumption habits to save money.

Again, our point is not that you should live a miserable life of austerity and sacrifice so that you can be rich when you retire. Where's the advantage in becoming rich in the future by living in poverty until the future arrives? Instead, we are stressing that ordinary people can have a high standard of living and still accumulate a lot of wealth because it does not take much savings to get a big payoff. Of the $1,193,512 Roger accumulated by not smoking, only $139,613 came from reducing his consumption. Indeed, people who save and invest will be able to consume far more than those who do not. At retirement—or sooner—Roger can start spending his wealth and end up having much more than if he had never saved.

All it takes is an early savings program, a little patience, knowing how to get a reasonable return on your savings (see the next two elements), and taking advantage of the power of compound interest.

8. Diversify—don't put all your eggs in one basket.

The two most common financial assets are stocks and bonds. Let's make sure you understand the nature of these two instruments. **Stocks** represent ownership of corporate businesses. Stock owners are entitled to the fraction of the firm's future revenues represented by their ownership shares. If the business generates attractive future revenues, the stockholders will gain. The gains of stockholders typically come in the form of either dividends (regular payments to owners) or appreciation in the value of the stock. But, there is no assurance the business will be successful and earn income in the future. If unsuccessful, the value of the firm's stock will decline. While the stockholders are not liable for the debts of the corporation, they may lose all of the funds used to purchase the stock. (Note: "Equity" is another term for stock.)

Bonds provide businesses, governments, and other organizations with a convenient way to borrow money. These organizations acquire funds from bond purchasers in exchange for the promise (and legal obligation) to pay interest and repay the entire **principal** (amount borrowed) at specified times in the future. As long as the organization issuing the bond is solvent, the bondholder can count on the funds being repaid with interest.

All investments involve risk. The market value of a corporate stock investment can change dramatically in a relatively short period of time. Even if the **nominal return** is guaranteed, as in the case of high-quality bonds, changes in interest and/or inflation rates can substantially change the value of the asset. If you have most of your wealth tied up in ownership of a small number of corporate stocks (or even worse, a single stock), you are especially vulnerable. The recent experiences of those holding a large share of their assets in the **equities** of firms such as Enron, Bear Stearns, and Lehman Brothers illustrate this point.

You can reduce your risk through **diversification**—holding a large number of unrelated assets. Diversification puts the law of large numbers to work for you. While some of the investments in a diversified **portfolio** will do poorly, others will do extremely well. The performance of the latter will offset that of the former, and the rate of return will converge toward the average.

For those seeking to build wealth without having to become involved in day-to-day business decision-making, the stock market can provide attractive returns. It has done so historically. During the last two centuries, corporate stocks yielded a real rate of return (real means adjusted for inflation) of approximately 7 percent per year, compared to a real rate of return of about 3 percent for bonds.[11]

The risk with stocks is that no one can ever be sure what they will be worth at any specified time in the future; inevitably there will be periods over which the market value of your investments is falling, only to rise months or years later. But that risk, known as volatility, is a big reason why stocks yield a significantly higher rate of return than saving accounts, money market certificates, and short-term government bonds, all of which guarantee you a given amount in the future. Since most people value the additional certainty in the yields that bonds and savings accounts provide over stocks, the average return on stocks has to be higher to attract investors away from their less risky counterparts with more predictable returns.

Mutual funds can help investors diversify and reduce risk. Mutual funds simply combine the funds of a group of investors and channel them into various categories of investments, such as stocks (equities), bonds, real estate, or treasury bills. Thus, there are a variety of mutual fund categories.

An **equity mutual fund** channels the funds of its investors into the stock of many firms. These funds provide even small investors with an economical way to achieve diversity and reduce risk. The risks of stock market investments are substantially lowered if one continually adds to or holds a diverse portfolio of stocks over a lengthy period of time, say thirty or thirty-five years. Historically, when a diverse set of stocks

---

11. A 7 percent real rate of return may not sound like much compared to what some stocks, such as Dell and Microsoft, have yielded. But a 7 percent compounded rate of return means that the value of your savings will double every ten years. In contrast, it will take thirty-five years to double your money at a 2 percent interest rate, the approximate after-tax return earned historically by savings accounts and money market mutual funds. Note: You can approximate the number of years it will take to double your funds at alternative interest rates by simply dividing the yield (the average annual return on your money) into seventy. This is sometimes referred to as the Rule of 70.

has been held over a lengthy time frame, the rate of return has been high and the variation in that return has been relatively small. Regular payments into an equity mutual fund holding a diverse set of stocks provide investors with a low-cost method of investing in the stocks market.

Diversification will reduce the volatility of investments in the stock market in two ways. First, when some firms do poorly, others do well. An oil price decline that causes lower profits in the oil industry will tend to boost profits in the airline industry because the cost of airline fuel will decline. When profits in the steel industry fall because steel prices decline, the lower steel prices will tend to boost the profits in the automobile industry.

Second, diversification can help protect you against a change in general economic conditions. A recession or an expansion will cause changes in the value of the stocks of almost all firms. But diversification reduces the volatility in the value of your investments because a recession is worse for some firms and industries than others, and a boom is better for some than for others. For example, the recession that harms Nieman Marcus may boost sales and profits for Walmart, at least relative to most firms.

Some employers offer retirement programs—such as a 401(k) plan— that will match your purchases of the company stock (but not investments in other firms) or will allow you to purchase the company stock at a substantial discount. Such a plan makes purchasing the stock of your company attractive. If you have substantial confidence in the company, you may want to take advantage of this offer. After a holding period, typically three years, these plans will permit you to sell the purchased shares and use the proceeds to undertake other investments. As soon as you are permitted to do so, you should choose this option. Failure to do so will mean that you will soon have too many of your investment eggs in the basket of the company for which you work. This places you in a position of double jeopardy: Both your employment and the value of your investments depend substantially on the success of your employer. Do not put yourself in this position.

We can summarize the importance of stock investments and diversity this way: To achieve their financial potential, individuals must channel their savings into diversified investments that yield attractive returns. In the past, long-term investments in the stock market have yielded high returns. Equity mutual funds make it possible for even small investors to hold a diverse portfolio, add to it monthly, and still keep transaction costs low. Investing in a diverse portfolio over a lengthy period of time reduces the risk of stock ownership to a low level. All investments have some uncertainty. But if the past century and a half are any guide, we can confidently expect that over the long haul, a diverse portfolio of corporate stocks will yield a higher real return than will savings accounts, bonds, certificates of deposit, money market funds, and similar financial instruments. Ownership of stock through mutual funds is particularly attractive for young people saving for their retirement years.

9. Indexed equity mutual funds can help you beat the experts without taking excessive risk.

Many Americans refrain from investments in stocks because they feel they do not have either the time or expertise to identify businesses that are likely to be successful in the future. They are correct about the difficulties involved in forecasting the future direction of either individual stocks or a broad measure of their average price. No one can say for sure what will happen to either the price of any specific stock or the general level of stock prices in the future.

Most economists accept the **random walk theory**. According to this theory, current stock prices reflect the best information that is known about the future state of corporate earnings, the health of the economy, and other factors that influence stock prices. Therefore future changes of stock prices will be driven by surprise occurrences, things that people do not currently anticipate. By their very nature, these factors are unpredictable. If they were predictable, they would already be reflected in current stock prices.

Why not pick just the stocks that will do well, as Apple, Google, and Microsoft have, and stay away from everything else? That is a great idea, except for one problem: The random walk theory also applies to the prices of specific stocks. The prices of stocks with attractive future profit potential will already reflect these prospects. The future price of a specific stock will be driven by unforeseen changes and additional information about the prospects of the firm that will only become known over time. Countless factors affect the future price of a particular stock, and they are constantly changing in unpredictable ways. The price of Apple stock could be driven down, for example, because of an idea a high-school kid is working on in his basement right now. Thus there is no way that you can know ahead of time which stocks are going to rocket into the financial stratosphere and which ones are going to fizzle on the launch pad or crash after takeoff.

You may be able to improve your chances a little by studying the stock market, the details of particular corporations, and economic trends and forecasts. For most of us, however, the best option will be to channel our long-term (that is, our retirement) savings into an equity mutual fund.

There are two broad categories of equity mutual funds: managed funds and indexed funds. A **managed equity mutual fund** is one in which an "expert," the fund's portfolio manager, decides what stocks will be held and when they will be bought and sold. The fund manager is almost always supported by a research staff that examines both individual companies and market trends in an effort to identify those stocks that are most likely to do well in the future. The manager seeks to pick and choose the stock holdings of the fund in a manner that will maximize the fund's rate of return.

The second type of fund, an **indexed equity mutual fund**, merely holds stocks in the same proportion as their representation in broad indexes of the stock market such as the S&P 500 or the Dow Jones Industrial Average. Very little trading is necessary to maintain a portfolio of stocks that mirrors a broad index. Neither is it necessary for index funds to undertake research evaluating the future prospects of companies. Because of these two factors, the operating costs of index funds are substantially lower, usually 1 or 2 percentage points lower, than those of managed funds. As a result, index funds charge lower fees and therefore a larger share of your investment flows directly into the purchase of stock.

An equity mutual fund indexed to a broad stock market indicator such as the S&P 500 will earn approximately the average stock market return for its shareholders. What is so great about the average return? As noted earlier, historically the stock market has yielded an average real rate of return of about 7 percent. That means that the real value, the value adjusted for inflation, of your stock holdings doubles approximately every ten years. That's not bad. Even more important, the average rate of return yielded by a broad index fund beats the return of almost all managed mutual funds when comparisons are made over periods of time such as a decade. This is not surprising because, as the random walk theory indicates, not even the experts will be able to forecast consistently the future direction of stock prices with any degree of accuracy.

Over the typical ten-year period, the S&P 500 has yielded a higher return than 85 percent of the actively managed funds. Over twenty-year periods, mutual funds indexed to the S&P 500 have generally outperformed about 98 percent of the actively managed funds.[12] Thus the odds are very low, about one in fifty, that you or anyone else will be

---

12. See Jeremy J. Siegal, *Stocks for the Long Run,* 3rd edition (New York: McGraw Hill, 2002): 342–43.

able to select an actively managed fund that will do better than the market average *over the long run*.

Just because a managed mutual fund does well for a few years or even a decade, it does not follow that it will do well in the future. For example, the top twenty managed equity funds during the 1980s outperformed the S&P 500 Index by 3.9 percentage points per year over the decade. But if investors entering the market in 1990 thought they would beat the market by choosing the "hot" funds of the 1980s, they would have been disappointed. The top twenty funds of the 1980s underperformed the S&P 500 Index by 1.2 percentage points per year during the 1990s. Similarly, the average return of the top twenty managed equity funds from 1990 to 1999 outperformed the S&P 500 Index by 3.1 percentage points per year, but from 2000 to 2009 those same funds underperformed the S&P 500 Index by 1.3 percentage points per year.[13]

The "hot" funds during the stock market bubble of the late 1990s were an even more misleading investment indicator. Over the two-year period 1998–1999 the top-performing managed fund was Van Wagoner Emerging Growth, with a 105.52 percent average annual return. But over the two-year period 2000–2001, this fund experienced an average annual return of *minus* 43.54 percent, one of the lowest during this period.[14]

These examples actually understate the advantage of a mutual fund indexed to the S&P 500 compared to a managed equity fund because of the survivorship bias. The S&P 500 index is highly unlikely to go out of business, but over the time period relevant to saving for retirement, a managed fund is quite likely to shut down. A mutual fund can disappear

13. See Burton Malkiel, *A Random Walk Down Wall Street: The Time Tested Strategy for Successful Investing* (New York: W. W. Norton & Company, 2015): 177–78

14. See Burton G. Malkiel, *A Random Walk Down Wall Street: The Time-Tested Strategy for Successful Investing* (New York: W. W. Norton & Company, 2003): 189–190. For additional evidence that a mutual fund yielding a high rate of return during one period cannot be counted on to continue to do so in the future, see Mark M. Carhart, "On Persistence in Mutual Fund Performance," *The Journal of Finance* 52, No. 1 (March 1997): 57–82.

for two reasons, both related to poor performance. It may be shut down with the remaining value of the fund distributed to its owners, or may be merged into another managed fund with a better record. Although there are thousands of managed mutual funds today, in 1970 there were only 358. Burton Malkiel followed those funds through 2013. During these 43 years, 274 funds—over 75 percent of the total—ceased to exist. Out of the remaining 84, only 4 had outperformed the S&P 500 index by 2 percentage points or more on an annual basis.[15]

The stock market has historically yielded higher returns than other major investment categories, and index funds make it possible for the ordinary investor to earn these returns without worrying about trying to pick either individual stocks or a specific mutual fund. Of course there will be ups and downs and even some fairly lengthy periods of declining stock prices. Therefore many investors will want to reduce equities as a percentage of their asset holdings as they approach retirement (see the following element). But based on a lengthy history of stock market performance, the long-term yield derived from a broad index of the stock market can be expected to exceed that of any other alternative, including managed equity funds.[16]

As Exhibit 14 illustrates, when held over a lengthy time period, a diverse holding of stocks has historically yielded both a high and relatively stable rate of return. Data for the highest and lowest average annual real rate of return (the return adjusted for inflation) derived from broad stock market investments for periods of varying length between the years 1871 and 2014 are shown here. The exhibit assumes that the investor paid a fixed amount annually into a mutual fund that mirrored the S&P 500

15. See Burton G. Malkiel, *A Random Walk Down Wall Street: The Time-Tested Strategy for Successful Investing* (New York: W. W. Norton & Company, 2003): 180–81.
16. Even those investing in index funds should obtain some advice from experts. There are tax and legal considerations such as taking advantage of tax-deferred possibilities, establishing wills and trusts, making wise insurance choices, etc., which do require input from specialists.

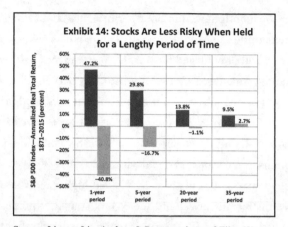

Source: Linqun Liu, Andrew J. Rettenmaier, and Zijun Wang, "Social Security and Market Risk," National Center for Policy Analysis Working Paper Number 244 (July 2001). The returns are based on the assumption that an individual invests a fixed amount for each year in the investment period. Data are updated through 2015.

Index.[17] Clearly, huge swings are possible when stocks are held for only a short time period. During the 1871–2014 period, the single-year returns of the S&P 500 ranged from 47.2 percent to minus 40.8 percent. Even over a five-year period, the compound annual returns ranged from 29.8 percent to minus 16.7 percent.

However, note how the "best returns" and "worst returns" converge as the length of the investment period increases. When a thirty-five-year period is considered, the compound annual return for the best thirty-five years between 1871 and 2014 was 9.5 percent, compared to 2.7 percent for the worst thirty-five years. Thus, the annual real return of stocks during the worst-case scenario was about the same as the real return for bonds. This high and relatively stable long-term return makes stocks a particularly attractive method of saving for retirement.

17. See Liqun Liu, Andrew J. Rettenmaier, and Zijun Wang, "Social Security and Market Risk," National Center for Policy Analysis Working Paper, No. 244, July 2001.

Here is the most important takeaway from this element: Do not allow a lack of time and expertise to keep you out of equity investments. You do not have to do a lot of research or be a "super stock picker" in order to be a successful investor. Regular contributions into an indexed equity mutual fund will provide you with attractive returns on long-term investments with minimal risk. For most, these investments will be an important ingredient of a sound retirement plan. Every large reputable investment firm will have several indexed equity mutual funds from which to choose. Each firm may have a slightly different name for its fund so be sure to read the description to determine the one that best fits your needs.

10. *Invest in stocks for long-run objectives, but as the need for money approaches, increase the proportion of bonds.*

When making long-term investments, such as the funds allocated into a retirement plan, a stock index fund is generally your best investment. While the long-term return of stocks is substantially greater than bonds, the value of the latter is more stable over short time periods. As the time approaches when the funds from an investment plan may be needed, it will make sense to shift funds toward investments of more stable value. Given a five-year horizon, purchasing a bond that matures in five years, at which point you will receive your initial investment plus interest, is a relatively safe investment. As a general proposition, buy bonds that mature at about the time you will need the funds, perhaps for a down payment on a home or income during retirement.

The greatest risk of owning bonds is inflation, which lessens the value of both the principal and the fixed-interest payments. However, that risk can be reduced or eliminated with the use of **TIPS,** or **Treasury Inflation-Protected Securities.** This product is a form of a U.S. Treasury bond that was first sold in 1997. TIPS return the principal, a fixed-interest rate that depends on the market rate when they are purchased, and an additional payment to adjust for inflation. Because unanticipated inflation is what causes the return from bonds to be worth less than expected, buying and holding TIPS will protect the holder against that risk. TIPS are particularly attractive for retirees seeking to generate a specific stream of real purchasing power from their assets.

An additional risk associated with bonds is the impact of changes in interest rates. Suppose you buy a $1,000, thirty-year bond that pays 5 percent interest. This bond promises to pay you $50 in interest every year for thirty years, at which time it matures and you get $1,000. But if the overall or general interest rate increases to 10 percent soon after you buy this bond, then your bond will immediately fall in value to about one-half of what you paid for it. The reason? At a 10 percent interest rate, an investor can get $50 in interest every year by buying a $500 bond. So $500 is about all anyone will be willing to pay for your $1,000 bond. Of course if the interest rate drops to 2.5 percent soon after you buy your thirty-year 5 percent bond, then its price will approximately *double* in value. But this is more volatility (or risk) than you want to take if you are saving for something you expect to buy in five years.

How long should a portfolio consist of stocks, and when should the move to bonds be made? That depends on the length of time before you want to access the investment funds. As we suggested above, relatively short-term investments may do best in bonds exclusively. For example, a young couple saving in order to place 20 percent down to buy a house may be better off avoiding the stock market entirely—for that portion of their savings *only*—and investing it in bonds. That is because purchasing a house or condominium often involves saving for just a few years. In contrast, a couple might save for eighteen years to finance a college education for a newborn or thirty-five to forty-five years to build up savings for their retirement. In these two cases, equities should be an important part of, or perhaps the entire, investment fund for most of the saving years.

The parents of a newborn who begin saving right away for the child's college education have more years to build wealth and to diversify the risk of capitalizing on stocks to build it faster. In that case, having some of that college portfolio in equities may make sense. However, as the plunge in stock prices during the Great Recession of 2008–2009 illustrates, even with an eighteen-year horizon, stock holdings involve risk. Again, investors seeking to reduce risk in their college funds can do so by holding fewer stocks and more bonds, especially as the time approaches when the funds will be needed.

As people earn more and live longer, saving for retirement expenses becomes ever more important. We don't want to drastically, and negatively, alter our lifestyle upon retirement and we cannot afford to outlive our retirement nest eggs. For the saver whose retirement is more than ten years ahead, a diversified portfolio of stocks, such as a mutual fund indexed to the S&P 500, probably makes the best investment portfolio. For the more conservative saver, having 10, 20, or even 40 percent of one's portfolio in bonds will generally provide more stability in the value of one's retirement assets, even though total returns will probably be lower in the end.

As the need for retirement income approaches, it is prudent for all but the most wealthy among us to begin to switch an all-stock portfolio gradually into bonds. When that switch should begin depends partly on when and how much monthly income is needed during retirement. For those individuals with a large portfolio or a good pension income relative to their retirement income needs, much of their savings can be left longer in equities to maximize expected total return. The goal of switching to bonds is primarily to avoid the need to sell stocks at temporarily low prices. The sooner you expect to turn to your portfolio to meet monthly living expenses, the more important it is to reduce risk by moving strategically and gradually into bonds.

With regard to retirement investments, it is also vitally important to consider the tax treatment of both your investment contributions and retirement income. There are two broad types of retirement plans: traditional plans and Roth IRA plans. Traditional plans include Individual Retirement Accounts (IRA), 401(k) plans offered by employers, and equivalent 403(b) plans provided by nonprofit organizations. For traditional plans, the contributions into retirement investment accounts are deductible against your taxable income at the time of the contribution. Thus, your tax bill during the current year will be lower. As the result of the tax saving during the current year, your after-tax income will fall by less than your contribution into the traditional plan. In such plans, the taxes on the contributions into your retirement account, as well as the earnings from these investments, are cast into the future. That is, they are tax-deferred until they are withdrawn during retirement. This will be particularly advantageous if you expect to be in a lower tax bracket during your retirement years.

In contrast, the contributions into a Roth IRA are not tax deductible. Thus, there is no tax advantage at the time the contributions are made. However, the value of your investments grow tax-free in Roth IRAs. Thus, during your retirement years, both the contributions and investment earnings of a Roth IRA can be withdrawn without any payment of taxes.

Summarizing, the value of Roth IRA investments grows tax-free while the contributions and earnings from traditional plans are tax-deferred. Under certain conditions a tax break in the future can more than make up for the fact that your after-tax income during your working years will be less with a Roth than with a traditional IRA or 401(k). At first glance, a Roth IRA will probably be better for you if you believe your current marginal income tax rate is about the same or lower than what you expect it to be when you are making withdrawals during retirement. In contrast, a traditional IRA or 401(k) will generally be a better option if you believe your current tax rate is higher than it is likely to be during your retirement years. Nonetheless, factors other than present and future income (and tax rates) can be also important, which is why you should seek some impartial and expert advice before making a decision.

Our advice to those seeking to prepare for future retirement can be summed up this way: Start saving for retirement early, stay with diversified portfolios of stocks until the need for funds is near enough in time to justify gradual shifts toward lower-risk, lower-return assets such as bonds, and take advantage of the favorable tax treatment provided for retirement plans.

11. *Take steps that will reduce risk when making housing, education, and other investment decisions.*

The purchase of a home is one of the most important decisions most of us will confront during our lifetime. For most, a home purchase will be their largest investment, at least initially. Buying a home you can afford in a desirable location and keeping it well-maintained can be a good investment. But, as the housing crisis of 2008–2009 illustrates, there are potential pitfalls. Examination of the following factors will help you avoid the worst problems.

First, carefully consider the "own versus rent" option. Many people immediately conclude that purchasing is a better option than renting because purchasing can build home equity. They reason that their money is wasted on rent going into the landlord's pocket when it could be put to work creating equity, helping to build the homeowner's net worth as the mortgage is paid off and the market value of the property appreciates. However, during the first few years of a mortgage, almost all of the monthly payment is for interest and very little is actually building equity. So if you sell the house within three years, for example, you will have accumulated little or no equity. You've simply paid the bank interest instead of paying rent to a landlord.

Second, buying and selling real estate is expensive and therefore it is not a good idea to purchase a house unless you expect to live in it at least three years. In most states, realtor commissions are 6 percent or more of the sale price. Closing costs on a mortgage are typically several thousand dollars. If you sell the house within a few years after the initial purchase, the transaction costs are likely to be greater than your equity.

Third, do not buy a house until you have saved for a 20 percent down payment. If your down payment is less than 20 percent, you will have to pay mortgage insurance, which increases your monthly payment. (Mortgage insurance protects the lender from losses that occur when a person defaults on payments.) Also, do not use a mortgage with a low "teaser interest rate" to purchase your home. These rates are followed by sharply escalating interest rates, which will substantially increase your monthly mortgage payment after the initial period has expired.

Fourth, just because you can afford a mortgage payment doesn't mean you can afford the house. The mortgage is the first and most obvious payment made each month. However, housing requires other regular payments and obligations that you need to consider. If they are not included in the mortgage as escrow, property taxes must be paid. Homeowner's insurance is required. The roof may leak one day, the hot water heater, dishwasher, or clothes dryer may break down, the air conditioning unit or plumbing system may need repair, or any number of other items may result in maintenance costs. You will need a lawn mower and other equipment to maintain your yard. These are all regular expenses you can expect as a home owner. You need to factor them into your monthly budget when examining whether home ownership makes sense for you.

Lastly, as you build up equity in your house, do not take out another mortgage or borrow against your equity in order to increase your current consumption. Housing prices go down as well as up. After the housing crisis of 2008–2009, many people were "upside down" or "under water" with their housing. That is, the appraised value of their home was less than the outstanding mortgage. Some people incurred huge losses when they sold their home. Others simply couldn't afford to sell at a loss and kept the home, hoping for a market rebound. Still others went through the painful process of foreclosure. Thus, safety dictates that it is important to maintain a sizeable equity in your home.

Living by the guidelines presented above will encourage you to live within your means, economize on housing, and minimize the risks involved in housing decisions. Now, let's turn to investments in education.

For many people, postsecondary education—that is, education beyond high school—provides an attractive investment opportunity. However, it is not for everyone. Going to college is costly. If a student incurs the time and money cost of going to college for a couple of years, then drops out without a diploma, the investment is unlikely to be a profitable one. The biggest risk for a student considering postsecondary education is the possibility of a negative return on his or her investment. This would occur if the higher earnings achieved from the education are less than the costs involved in obtaining the education.

According to the Bureau of Labor Statistics (BLS), the median annual earnings in 2014 for workers holding bachelor's degrees were over $20,000 higher than for those who only had a high school diploma.[18] But there is substantial variation in the earnings of college graduates. The actual earnings after graduation depend on many factors, including the skills acquired, college major, and the overall demand and supply conditions of a particular labor market. According to PayScale.com, which has compiled the world's largest database of salary profiles, the college majors with the highest earnings potential include engineering, actuarial and applied mathematics, computer science, physics, statistics, economics, and management information systems. Majors with low earnings

---

18. U.S. Department of Labor, Bureau of Labor Statistics (2015, April 2). *Employment Projections*. Retrieved from: www.bls.gov/emp/ep_chart_001.htm.

potential include child and family studies, education, social work, exercise science, athletic training, music, and culinary arts.[19]

It is risky to borrow a large sum of money to finance an education expected to result in low future earnings. As we indicated in Part 4, Elements 1 and 2, it is important to choose a work activity that you enjoy. But, your choice needs to be well-informed. Search for and discover the expected earnings in the occupations for which you are training. We want you to make informed choices that will lead to the largest possible return on your educational investment—including the personal satisfaction you derive from the employment.

Let's consider why students sometimes choose educational options that result in negative returns. First, many students have unrealistic expectations about future income. With inflated expectations, they may be willing to pay more for their education than what their future income can support. You should investigate resources to keep informed of labor market conditions and earnings potential. In addition to PayScale.com, the BLS Occupational Outlook Handbook (*OOH*) is a valuable source. This online handbook provides information on hundreds of occupations, including their requirements, job outlook and growth prospects, and median pay. Having realistic expectations about future income is a vital ingredient in making better decisions about postsecondary education.

Second, many students underestimate the cost of education. The total cost of education includes the direct cost of tuition, books, fees, and room and board, but don't forget about opportunity costs. Going to school, even part-time, means giving up current income from a job. Make sure to properly account for the total cost of education.

Third, students overuse debt. Some view the student loan check as free money and borrow too much. Many young people are ill-prepared to

19. Pay Scale, Inc. *College Salary Report 2015–2016*. Retrieved from www.payscale .com/college-salary-report/majors-that-pay-you-back/bachelors.

judge how difficult it will be to squeeze the funds for repayment of student loans out of their monthly budget after graduation. Assuming a 3 percent interest rate, you will pay $345.29 per month for fifteen years to repay $50,000 in loans. You will pay $517.94 per month for fifteen years to repay $75,000 and $690.58 per month to repay $100,000. Will your future earnings be sufficient to make the monthly payment on your student loans within the context of your overall budget? Think seriously about this issue prior to taking out a student loan.

We are not saying that you should never borrow to finance education. There are times when this option makes sense. Like any other form of debt, student loan debt requires repayment of principal plus interest and fees. A variety of student loan programs exist. Investigate them carefully to decide what's best for you.

To further minimize education risks, students and their parents can pursue other options to finance education. As a general guideline, develop a financial plan that has debt as the last option. Start with a college savings plan. Parents, relatives, and friends can start their own savings plans or consider the relative benefits of contributing to a government-sponsored Qualified Tuition Program. These programs come in two forms. The first is a prepaid tuition plan, which allow participants to pay a predetermined tuition amount for future education. The second is an investment plan (referred to as a 529 plan) usually comprised of mutual funds, where withdrawals made for qualified educational expenses are tax-free.

Scholarships and grants are also available. They are particularly attractive because they do not have to be repaid. High school guidance offices and the Internet are loaded with scholarship and grant lists. Make time to search for them. Each will have a specific set of instructions, eligibility requirements, and deadlines. Factor all of these options into your decision to invest in education and choose a path that makes sense for you given market considerations.

While housing and education are likely to be the largest investments you'll make, other investment opportunities will emerge. There are precautions to take when considering which ones to seize. It is important to recognize that when making investments, you are vulnerable; you must think about whether your interests are aligned with the party offering the investment. Whenever you are offered something that seems to be an extremely attractive proposition, it pays to step back and carefully examine the incentives behind why this proposition is being presented to you. Borrowers looking for money to finance a project will initially turn to low-cost sources such as bank loans. Finding individual investors like you and promising a high rate of return makes no sense if financing is available from bank lenders and other investment specialists. High potential returns on any investment inevitably come with high risk; that is, there is a high probability of failure. If banks and professional investors are not interested in the investment, you should ask yourself, "Why should I be?"

The interests of those selling investment alternatives are often substantially different than yours. While you want to earn an attractive return, they are likely to be primarily interested in the commission on the sale or earnings derived from management fees or a high salary related to the business venture. Put bluntly, their primary interest is served by getting their hands on your money. They do not necessarily seek to defraud you; they may well believe that the investment is a genuine opportunity with substantial earning potential. But no matter how nice they are, how well you know them, or how much it appears that they want to help you, their interests are different from yours. Moreover, once they have your money, you will be in a weak position to alter the situation.

How can you tell beforehand whether an investment is a wise one? There is no "silver bullet" that can assure positive results from all investment decisions. But there are things you can do that will help you avoid investment disasters costing you tens of thousands of dollars. The following six guidelines are particularly important.

1. If it looks too good to be true, it probably is. This is an old cliché, but a valid one. Some investment marketers may be willing to do just about anything to obtain your money because, once they do, they are in charge and you are vulnerable.

2. Deal only with parties that have a reputation to protect. Established companies with a solid reputation will be reluctant to direct their clients into unsound investments. For example, an initial public stock offering by an upstart brokerage firm with which only a few are familiar is far more likely to result in loss than the offering of an established firm with a substantial reputation on the line.

3. Never purchase an investment solicited by telephone or e-mail. Such marketing is a technique used by those looking to prey on those individuals who are easy targets. Do not let yourself be a victim of scams. Never share personal information with people you do not explicitly trust. Your social security number, date of birth, cell phone number, and postal address should be carefully guarded.

4. Do not allow yourself to be forced into a quick decision. Take time to develop an investment strategy. Never let yourself be pressured into a hasty decision.

5. Do not allow friendship to influence an investment decision. Numerous people have been directed into bad investments by their friends. If you want to keep a person as your friend, invest your money with an objective third party.

6. If high-pressure marketing is involved, grab your checkbook and run. Attractive investments are sold without the use of high-pressure marketing techniques. If you already have a substantial portfolio, there may be a place in it for high-risk investments, including **"junk" bonds** and precious metals. But those investments must come from funds that you can

afford to lose. If you are looking for a sound way to build wealth, most of your funds should be in more routine lower-risk investments helping you establish a well-diversified portfolio.

12. Use insurance to help manage risk.

Life involves risks. The risks of life range from the small and financially insignificant, like receiving poor service at a restaurant, to the large and financially devastating, such as a severe illness or having your home destroyed by a tornado. While you cannot eliminate risk, you can take steps to reduce and manage it.

You can make choices that will reduce risks. Not texting while driving reduces the chance of being involved in an accident. Wearing a seatbelt lowers the chance of injury if you are involved in a collision. Installing smoke detectors and a security system decreases the likelihood of your residence burning down or getting burglarized. Decreasing sugar consumption and eating low-cholesterol foods reduce the chance of illness and disease. However, while your choices can reduce risk, it cannot be eliminated.

How can you manage risk and protect yourself from the most adverse consequences? Insurance can reduce the financial loss resulting from damages to possessions (such as your home or car), an illness, loss of income, or other harmful events. Insurance provides a way for a group of people to pool payments and share risks in order to offset the losses of members actually damaged by an adverse event. The principle of sharing risk is often forgotten because individuals pay premiums to an insurance company and have no interaction with the group members. The insurance company is an intermediary, or middleman, in the risk-sharing process. The company collects premiums from each member of the group (its policyholders), then disburses payments when a covered loss occurs.

To understand how risk sharing works, imagine the following situation. You and four associates go to a restaurant for lunch and expect that the total bill will be $100. The five of you agree to instruct the waitress to randomly give the check to one of you at the end of the meal and that person will pay the entire amount. You and the other group members can then choose between two options: (1) take a chance, and hope you are not selected to pay the $100 bill; or (2) pay a premium of $20 to an insurer, who will pay the $100 bill if you are selected. Many people will prefer option 2 because it is less risky. While you have to pay the $20 premium, you protect yourself against the 20 percent possibility of having to pay the entire $100 bill.

Of course, insurers providing the risk-sharing service incur costs. They will have to assess risks, formalize agreements, collect premiums, examine and validate claims, and process payments. These handling and processing costs will have to be covered, in addition to the costs of the risk. Thus, the insurance premiums will have to be somewhat higher than the expected costs of the loss. For example, if an insurance company were going to provide members of our lunch group with protection against the 20 percent chance they might end up with the $100 bill, it would have to charge each a little more than $20, perhaps $22, in order to have an incentive to offer the service.

Insurance reduces risk because it spreads the burden of unfortunate events that a few experience over a larger group of people. In the lunch situation, the $100 bill is coming with certainty. The uncertainty comes from not knowing which member of the group will receive it. A larger group will increase the amount of the potential loss but it will also reduce the chance of any individual member receiving the bill.

When it comes to large sums, most of us are risk-averse. That means we are willing to pay a premium in order to reduce the adverse consequences of various events. Buying insurance is one way of reducing exposure to risks.

Insurance, however, is not always cost-effective. You should think carefully about whether it makes sense for you to insure against a risk. Yes, you should insure against events that, if they occur, will impose severe financial hardship. A severe illness that prevents you from working for an extended period of time, a car accident, or a flood that damages your home are examples. However, insuring against relatively small adverse events such as a breakdown of an appliance or television is generally not cost-effective. Providing the risk-sharing service will be expensive relative to the potential harm. Thus, it will generally be more economical to accept these risks and use a rainy day account (see Part 4, Element 6) to plan for and cover the cost of these risks. In contrast, automobile, housing, and healthcare insurance are usually cost-effective. In these cases, the cost of spreading the risks over a group of people is generally low relative to the potential damages of an adverse event. We now turn to those topics.

Most states require car owners to maintain some level of automobile insurance. Make sure to check with your insurance company so that you meet the minimum requirements. Customers will pay a premium based on a number of factors. Those include the driver's record, characteristics of the driver, the type of automobile, and the specific coverage limits and deductibles of the policy. A deductible is the amount the customer must pay first before any insurance coverage applies. For example, a $500 deductible means the customer must pay $500 before the insurance policy will pay for a loss. Generally, the higher the deductible the lower the premium. Coverage is the maximum amount the policy will pay in the event of a loss.

An auto policy is typically structured with a few basic coverages, or types of loss. Collision pays for damanges to your car in the event of an accident. Comprehensive pays for non-collison damages such as theft, vandalism, and acts of nature like a tree branch falling on your windshield. Liability coverage comes in two forms. First, it pays others for damages to their person or vehicle caused by the operation of your automobile. Second, it pays damages to you and your passengers for medical expenses and death benefits. For example, liability coverage of $500,000 means the most the insurance will pay in the event of a loss is $500,000, even if the actual loss is greater. When purchasing insurance, you should consider carefully the size of your coverage limits and deductible levels. Do you have enough in your rainy day account or other funds to pay the deductible?

As discussed in Part 4, Element 11, housing is the largest investment most people will make. It makes sense to insure against the loss of your biggest asset. All homeowners in the United States are required to have some level of insurance, mandated by state regulations or the financial institution holding a mortgage against the house (or both). Make sure to consult with your insurance company so that you are meeting the required minimum standards. Similar to auto policies, housing insurance will have deductibles and coverage limits. Housing insurance typically has three basic kinds of coverage. The first pays for damages to the house and other structures such as a detached garage or shed. The second pays for damages to the personal property of the homeowner—that is, the items inside the house. The third pays for liability. It covers other people who may get injured at your home. As in the case of auto insurance, if you choose a higher deductible, your premiums will generally be lower. You should carefully analyze how much risk to bear yourself.

Healthcare insurance can be a complicated issue because of the financing and payment methods for customers and the variety of plans available. Some people obtain their insurance through their employer while others buy directly from an insurance company. Some people pay all of their premiums while others have third parties pay (for example, the government or employer). Plans vary, including Health Maintenance Organizations (HMOs), Health Savings Accounts (HSAs), Preferred Provider Organizations (PPOs), Medicare, and Medicaid. In the United

States, the Patient Protection and Affordable Care Act, enacted by Congress in 2010, added further complexity by mandating broader coverage and implementing a system of taxes, penalties, and subsidies. In other countries, there is complete government control of the healthcare system. The complexities surrounding healthcare insurance and international comparisons of systems are beyond the scope of this book, but we want to make a few principles clear.

The payments made for healthcare insurance come in four forms. First, premiums (or taxes) are paid to obtain the coverage offered by the plan. Second, a deductible may apply. Third, there is the copay, which is a fee for a particular service such as a doctor office visit or prescription. Copays typically range from $10 to $100. Fourth, coinsurance is the percent of the medical bill the customer must pay. For example, a plan may require the customer to pay 20 percent of the bill for a hospital stay or medical procedure.

Competition in healthcare insurance is generally more restricted than for other forms of insurance, which means consumers will have fewer options available. Also, unlike most other insurance, consumers typically can make changes to their plan only once a year. This makes it more difficult to put together a plan that meets your needs. You may be forced into some coverage for a period of time that you don't want or cannot use. Even with these restrictions, you will have some choices to make about how much risk to assume yourself and how much you can share with others.

There are circumstances where having insurance protection actually increases risk. This is known as **moral hazard**. Consider the following two scenarios. Rachel trades in her twelve-year-old car and buys the most recent model, which has all the latest technological advances and safety devices. Since Rachel feels safer in the new car, she might actually drive a little less carefully knowing that her chance of becoming injured in a collision is less because of the safety devices. Jacob's mother insists he wears a helmet, knee and elbow pads, and long pants when he rides his skateboard. Embolded with a sense of security and protection, Jacob might attempt more dangerous jumps and maneuvers on his skateboard knowing that an injury is less likely. Under both scenarios, the risk increases because of the change in behavior from feeling safer.

Other types of insurance to consider, but not covered here, include life, disability, and long-term care. After evaluating your personal choices that determine the level of risk in your life, carefully analyze the risks you cannot avoid but can reduce through the effective use of insurance. It makes sense to insure against risks with large potential adverse effects, but when the potential financial damages are small, it is generally best to either absorb their cost in your monthly budget or cover them with funds from your rainy day account. The most important objective of an insurance strategy is to prevent devastating financial losses.

Concluding Thoughts

Besides being economists and educators, all of the authors are also parents. In addition to leaving a legacy of knowledge to our students and other readers of this book, we wish to positively influence our children's lives. We encourage you to do the same.

Parents want their children to be successful, not just financially, but in all aspects of life. Financial security tends to elevate general well-being by making necessities attainable and eliminating worry about fulfilling basic needs. Those who develop the habits of working diligently, setting goals and achieving them, and avoiding the temptations of instant gratification by considering the future consequences of current choices are typically more successful in all walks of life than those who don't. There are many ways to instill these attributes in your children. Getting them started on an earnings and savings program at an early age is one of them.

One of the most important ways to teach young people responsibility is by helping them understand that money is earned; it is not manna from heaven. Instead of just giving your children an allowance, pay them for performing certain tasks around the house and for achieving educational goals. Couple these payments with some discussion explaining that the money you earn is a measure of how well you help others. Money is not just a means of getting more of what you want, it is also a measure of your contribution in helping others get more of what *they* want. The best way to earn more money is by serving others and finding ways to make them better off. This entrepreneurial lesson will pay important dividends during your children's careers, no matter what those careers turn out to be.

Of course, you will buy your children many things without requiring that they earn the money for them. But even when you are paying for your children's purchases, it is possible to provide them with an understanding of the costs and trade-offs that are inherent in all expenditures. Throughout their lives, all of our children will have to decide how they are going to spend a limited income. If they spend more on one item, they will have to spend less on others. We all have to make trade-offs. Beginning at an early age, we need to teach our children about this reality and provide them with experiences that will help them learn to choose wisely.

To a large degree success in life is about setting goals, working hard to achieve them, figuring out how to make your services useful to others, saving for a specific purpose, and spending money wisely. These are the key ingredients for success. Economics provides the recipe for how to live a more fulfilling life.

We are now at the end of a journey. Throughout this book, our goal has been to provide you with information and tools that will help you live a more successful life. It is our hope that today you will start on a new journey—that you will earnestly resolve to take control of your life and choose options more consistent with success.

Acknowledgments

The authors would like to express their appreciation to several key people who contributed to this project. We owe a major debt to Jane Shaw Stroup, who edited the entire manuscript and made numerous modifications that improved both the content and readability. Signè Thomas helped with the preparation of the exhibits and provided research assistance throughout. Numerous comments from fellow teachers, college instructors, and economic educators are incorporated into the text. Special thanks of appreciation are extended to John Morton, Scott Niederjohn, Mark Schug, William Wood, Joe Connors, and Pam Cooper for their contributions to the development of new supplementary materials. Additionally, Brandon Brice, Joab Corey, Rosemarie Fike, Nathan Fowler, Fred Fransen, Mike Hammock, John Kessler, and Kelly Markson made contributions that enhanced content relevance, introduced new examples, and strengthened the electronic package accompanying this book. We would also like to express our appreciation to Tim Bartlett and Claire Lampen of St. Martin's Press, for their helpful comments and handling of the editorial responsibilities.

Through the years, the authors have had approximately forty

thousand students in our classes. Numerous discussions with students, both in and outside of class, have provided us with meaningful insights and presented us with challenging questions. Both have provided the foundation for this project. We cherish these interactions and dedicate the book to these students who have and continue to enrich our lives.

Digital Assets, Supplemental Units, and Website

For anyone who would like more readings and resources, a host of items are available at CommonSenseEconomics.com.

For instructors officially adopting the Common Sense Economics textbook for their course, an electronic package of assets is available. It includes a flexible course shell, learning objectives tied to national standards, PowerPoint slides, readings, audios, videos, discussion questions, and assessment items. The package is structured around the four parts of the book and is broken down into fifteen core modules, one for each week of a normal semester. Everything is ready to transfer to various course management systems, including Canvas, Moodle 2.9 or higher, and Blackboard. Visit CommonSenseEconomics.com/adopt to begin the formal adoption process.

For instructors who would like more coverage and additional details on key topics, the Common Sense Economics team has developed a series of supplementary modules. The readings for these modules are available at Common SenseEconomics.com/supplementals. An electronic package is also available for these supplements, which are listed below.

Module A: Demand, Supply, and Adjustments to Dynamic Change
Module B: Macroeconomic Indicators
Module C: Fiscal and Monetary Policy
Module D: The Great Depression and the Great Recession

Module E: Economics, Work, and Happiness
Module F: Economics, Markets, and Morality
Module G: The Economics of Poverty
Module H: Economics of the Environment
Module I: Smart Choices for Earning More Income
Module J: Smart Choices for Managing Credit
Module K: Smart Choices for Saving and Investing
Module L: Smart Choices for Insurance

Suggested Additional Readings

Acemoglu, Daron, and James A. Robinson. *Why Nations Fail: The Origins of Power, Prosperity, and Poverty.* New York: Crown, 2012.

Boettke, Peter. *Living Economics: Yesterday, Today, and Tomorrow.* Oakland, CA: Independent Institute, 2012.

Brooks, Arthur. *Gross National Happiness: Why Happiness Matters for America—and How We Can Get More of It.* New York: Basic Books, 2008.

Council on Economic Education. *Learning, Earning and Investing.* New York: 2004.

———. *Virtual Economics 4.5.* New York: 2014.

de Soto, Hernando. *The Mystery of Capital.* New York: Basic Books, 2000.

Folsom, Burton. *New Deal or Raw Deal?* New York: Simon & Schuster, 2008.

Friedman, Milton. *Capitalism and Freedom.* Chicago: University of Chicago Press, 2002.

Friedman, Milton, and Rose Friedman. *Free to Choose.* New York: Harcourt Brace Jovanovich, 1980.

Gwartney, James D., Richard L. Stroup, Russell S. Sobel, and David A. MacPherson. *Economics: Private and Public Choice,* 15th edition. Mason, OH: South-Western Cengage, 2014.

Gwartney, James D., Robert Lawson and Joshua Hall. *Economic Freedom of the World, 2015 Annual Report.* Vancouver: Fraser Institute, 2015.

Haskins, Ron, and Isabel V. Sawhill. *Creating an Opportunity Society.* Washington, D.C.: Brookings Institution Press, 2009.

Hayek, Friedrich. *Nobel Prize Lecture: The Pretence of Knowledge.* 1974. Available online: www.nobelprize.org/nobel_prizes/economic-sciences/laureates/1974/hayek-lecture.html.

Hazlitt, Henry. *Economics in One Lesson.* New Rochelle, New York: Arlington House, 1979.

Henderson, David R. (ed.) *Concise Encyclopedia of Economics.* Indianapolis: Liberty Fund, Available online: www.econlib.org/library/CEE.html.

Lee, Dwight R., and Richard B. McKenzie. *Getting Rich in America.* New York: Harper Business, 1999.

Malkiel, Burton. *A Random Walk Down Wall Street.* New York: W. W. Norton & Company, 2015.

Norberg, Johan. *Financial Fiasco: How America's Infatuation with Home Ownership and Easy Money Created the Economic Crisis.* Washington, D.C.: Cato Institute, 2009.

North, Douglass C. *Institutions, Institutional Change, and Economic Performance.* Cambridge: Cambridge University Press, 1990.

Rosenberg, Nathan, and L. E. Birdzell. *How the West Grew Rich.* New York: Basic Books, 1986.

Schug, Mark C., and William C. Wood. *Economic Episodes in American History.* Morristown, NJ: Wohl Publishing, Inc., 2011.

Shlaes, Amity. *The Forgotten Man: A New History of the Great Depression.* New York: Harper Perennial, 2008.

Smith, Adam. *The Theory of Moral Sentiments.* 1759. Library of Economics and Liberty. Available at: www.econlib.org/library/Smith/smMS.html.

———. *An Inquiry into the Nature and Causes of the Wealth of Nations.* 1776. Library of Economics and Liberty. Available online at: www.econlib.org/library/Smith/smWN.html.

Sowell, Thomas. *The Housing Boom and Bust,* New York: Basic Books, 2009.

———. *Basic Economics: A Common Sense Guide to the Economy*, 5th edition. New York: Basic Books, 2014.

Glossary

adjustable rate mortgage (ARMs): A home loan in which the interest rate, and thus the monthly payment, is tied to a short-term rate like the one-year Treasury bill rate. Typically, the mortgage interest rate will be two or three percentage points above the related short-term rate. It will be reset at various time intervals (e.g., annually) and thus the interest rate and monthly payment will vary over the life of the loan.

Alt-A loans: Loans extended with little documentation and or verification of the borrowers' income, employment, and other indicators of their ability to repay. Because of this poor documentation, these loans are risky.

average tax rate: The ratio of the total amount of taxes paid to total income.

balanced budget: The state of government finances when current government revenue from taxes, fees, and other sources is just equal to current government expenditures.

bond: A promise to repay the principal (amount borrowed) plus interest at a specified time in the future. Organizations such as corporations and governments issue bonds as a method of borrowing from bondholders.

budget (household): Estimated income and itemized planned expenditures for a time period.

budget deficit: The amount by which total government spending exceeds total government revenue during a specific time period, usually one year.

budget surplus: The amount by which total government spending falls below total government revenue during a specific time period, usually one year.

capital formation: The production of buildings, machinery, tools, and other equipment that will enhance future productivity. The term can also be applied to efforts to upgrade the knowledge and skill of workers (human capital) and thereby increase their ability to produce in the future.

capital inflow: The flow of expenditures on domestic stocks, bonds, and other assets undertaken by foreign investors.

capital investment: Expenditures on the buildings, machinery, tools, and other equipment that will enhance future productivity.

capital market: The broad term for the various marketplaces where investments such as stocks and bonds are bought and sold.

capital outflow: The flow of expenditures by domestic investors who are buying foreign stocks, bonds, and other assets.

cartel: An organization of sellers designed to coordinate supply and price decisions so that the joint profits of the members will be maximized. A cartel will seek to create a monopoly in the market for its product.

certification: Confirms the education, training, and other qualifications of an individual. Unlike licensing, certification does not prohibit noncertified individuals from competing in the market.

competition: A dynamic process of rivalry among parties such as producers or input suppliers, each of whom seeks to deliver a better deal to buyers when quality, price, and product information are all considered. Competition implies open entry into the market. Potential suppliers do not have to obtain permission from the government in order to enter the market.

complements: Products that enhance the value of each other and so tend to be used together. An increase in the price of one will cause a decrease in the demand for the other, and a decline in the price of one will cause an increase in the demand for the other (for example, sugar and coffee are complements, as are shoes and socks, and fast food and heartburn medication).

compound interest: Interest that is earned not only on the principal but also on the interest previously earned.

consumer price index (CPI): An indicator of the general level of prices. This government-issued index attempts to compare the cost of purchasing a market basket of goods bought by a typical consumer during a specific period with the cost of purchasing the same market basket during an earlier period.

creative destruction: The replacement of old products and production methods by innovative new ones that consumers judge to be more valuable. The process generates economic growth and higher living standards.

crony capitalism: A situation where the institutions of markets are maintained, but the allocation of resources, and the profit and loss of businesses, are substantially influenced by political decision-making rather than consumer purchases and market forces. To a large degree, the activities of business firms are directed and controlled by government subsidies, contracts, and regulations. In turn, many of the business firms will use contributions and other forms of political support to compete for government favors.

diversification: The strategy of investing in a number of diverse firms, industries, and instruments such as stocks, bonds, and real estate in order to minimize the risk accompanying investments.

division of labor: A method that breaks down the production of a commodity into a series of specific tasks, each performed by a different worker.

economic efficiency: A situation that occurs when (1) all activities generating more benefit than cost are undertaken; and (2) no activities are undertaken for which the cost exceeds the benefit.

economic institutions: The legal, regulatory, and monetary rules, laws, and customs that affect the security of property rights, enforcement of contracts, and the volume of exchange. They exert a major impact on transaction costs between parties, particularly when the trading partners do not know each other.

economic prosperity: Persistent increases in per capita income and improvements in the standard of living.

economies of scale: Reductions in the firm's per-unit costs that occur when large plants are used to produce large volumes of output.

economizing behavior: Choosing with the goal of gaining a specific benefit at the least possible cost. A corollary of economizing behavior implies that, when choosing among items of equal cost, individuals will choose the option that yields the greatest benefit.

equilibrium: A state in which the conflicting forces of supply and demand are in balance. When a market is in equilibrium, the decisions of consumers and producers are brought into harmony and quantity demanded will equal quantity supplied at the market clearing price.

equities: Shares of stock in a company. They represent fractional ownership of the company.

equity mutual fund: An entity that pools the funds of investors and uses them to purchase a bundle of stocks. Mutual funds make it possible for even small investors to hold a diverse bundle of stocks.

entrepreneur: A profit-seeking decision-maker who assumes the risk of developing innovative approaches and products with the expectation of realizing profits. A successful entrepreneur's actions will increase the value of resources.

exchange rate: The domestic price of one unit of a foreign currency. For example, if it takes $1.50 to purchase one English pound, the dollar-pound exchange rate is 1.50.

exports: Goods and services produced domestically but sold to foreign purchasers.

externalities: Spillover effects of an activity that influence the well-being of nonconsenting external parties. If the spillover effects are positive, they are also called external benefits. If the spillover effects adversely impact external parties, they are also called external costs.

FICO score: A mathematically determined score measuring a borrower's likely ability to repay a loan, similar to a credit score. The FICO score takes into account a borrower's payment history, current level of indebtedness, types of credit used and length of credit history, and new credit. A person's FICO score will range between 300 and 850. A score of 700 or more indicates the borrower's credit standing is good and therefore the risk of providing him or her with credit would be low. FICO is an acronym for the Fair Isaac Corporation, the creators of the FICO score.

foreclosure rate: The percentage of home mortgages on which the lender has started the process of taking ownership of the property because the borrower has failed to make the monthly payments.

foreign exchange market: The marketplaces in which the currencies of different countries are bought and sold.

government failure: A situation in which the structure of incentives is such that the political process, including democratic political decision-making, will encourage individuals to undertake actions that conflict with economic efficiency.

gross domestic product (GDP): The market value of all goods and services in their final (rather than intermediate) use that are produced within a country during a specific period. It is a measure of both income and output.

human capital: The abilities, skills, and health of human beings that contribute to the production of both current and future output. Investment in training and education can increase the supply of human capital.

incentives: The expected payoffs from actions. They may be either positive (the action is rewarded) or negative (the action results in penalty).

incentive structure: The types of rewards offered to encourage a certain course of action, and the types of factors intended to discourage alternative courses of action.

import quota: A specific limit or maximum quantity or value of a good that is permitted to be imported into a country during a given period.

imports: Goods and services produced by foreigners but purchased by domestic buyers.

income transfers: Payments made by the government to individuals and businesses that do not reflect services provided by the recipients. They are funds taxed away from some and transferred to others.

indexed equity mutual fund: An equity mutual fund that holds a portfolio of stocks that matches their share (or weight) in a broad stock market index such as the S&P 500. The overhead of these funds is usually quite low because their expenses on stock trading and research are low. The value of the mutual fund shares will move up and down along with the index to which the fund is linked.

inflation: A continuing rise in the general level of prices of goods and services. During inflation, the purchasing power of the monetary unit, such as the dollar, declines.

investment: The purchase, construction, or development of capital resources, including both nonhuman and human capital. Investments increase the supply of capital.

investment goods: Goods and/or facilities bought or constructed for the purpose of producing future economic benefits. Examples include rental houses, factories, ships, or roads. They are also often referred to as capital goods.

invisible hand: The tendency of market prices to direct individuals pursuing their own self-interest into activities that promote the economic well-being of the society.

"junk" bonds: High-risk bonds, usually issued by less-than-well-established firms, that pay high interest rates because of their risk.

law of comparative advantage: A principle that reveals how individuals, firms, regions, or nations can produce a larger output and achieve mutual gains from trade. Under this principle each specializes in the production of goods that it can produce cheaply (that is, at a low opportunity cost) and exchanges these goods for others that are produced at a high opportunity cost.

law of demand: A principle that states there is an inverse relationship between the price of an item and the quantity of it buyers are willing to purchase when other things are held constant. As the price of an item increases, consumers purchase less of it. As price decreases, they buy more.

law of supply: A principle that states there is a positive relationship between the price of an item and the quantity of it producers are willing to supply when other things are held constant. As the price of an item increases, producers will supply more. As price decreases, they will supply less.

less-developed countries: Countries with low per capita incomes, low levels of education, widespread illiteracy, and widespread use of production methods that are largely obsolete in high-income countries. They are sometimes referred to as developing countries.

liquid asset: An asset that can be easily and quickly converted to purchasing power without loss of value.

loanable funds market: A general term used to describe the broad market that coordinates the borrowing and lending decisions of business firms and households. Commercial banks, savings and loan associations, the stock and bond markets, and insurance companies are important financial institutions in this market.

logrolling: The exchange between politicians of political support on one issue for political support on another.

loss: The amount by which sales revenue fails to cover the cost of supplying a good or service. Losses are a penalty imposed on those who use resources to produce less value than they could have otherwise produced.

mal-investment: Mal-investment is misguided (or excess) investment caused when the Fed keeps interest rates artificially low, encouraging too much borrowing. The new bank credit is invested in capital projects that cost more than the value they create. At some point a correction must occur to cleanse these uneconomical investments from the system.

managed equity mutual fund: An equity mutual fund that has a portfolio manager who decides what stocks will be held in the fund and when they will be bought or sold. A research staff generally provides support for the fund manager.

marginal: A term used to describe the effects of a change in the current situation. For example, the marginal cost is the cost of producing an additional unit of a product, given the producer's current facility and production rate.

marginal benefit: The change in total value or benefit derived from an action such as consumption of an additional unit of a good or service. It reflects the maximum amount that the individual considering the action would be willing to pay for it.

marginal cost: The change in total cost resulting from an action such as the production of an additional unit of output.

marginal tax rate: The percentage of an extra dollar of income that must be paid in taxes. It is the marginal tax rate that is relevant in personal decision-making.

market: An abstract concept that encompasses the trading arrangements of buyers and sellers that underlie the forces of supply and demand.

market failure: A situation in which the structure of incentives is such that markets will encourage individuals to undertake activities that are inconsistent with economic efficiency.

market forces: The information and incentives communicated through market prices; profits and losses that motivate buyers and sellers to coordinate their decisions.

middlemen: People who buy and sell goods or services or arrange trades. Middlemen reduce transaction costs.

minimum wage: Legislation requiring that workers be paid at least the stated minimum hourly rate of pay.

monetary policy: The deliberate control of the national money supply and, in some cases, credit conditions, by the government. This policy establishes the environment for market exchange.

money: Anything that is generally accepted as final payment for goods and services by buyers and sellers; serves as a medium of exchange, a store of value, and a standard of value. Characteristics of money are portability, stability in value, uniformity, durability, and acceptance.

money interest rate: The interest rate measured in monetary units, often called the nominal interest rate. It overstates the real cost of borrowing during an inflationary period.

money supply: The supply of currency, checking account funds, and traveler's checks in a country. These items are counted as money because they are used as the means of payment for purchases.

monopoly: A market characterized by (1) a single seller of a well-defined product for which there are no good substitutes; and (2) high barriers to the entry of any other firms into the market for that product.

moral hazard: A situation where providing protection against a risk increases the occurrence of the risky behavior because it reduces the potential adverse consequences of the action.

mortgage: An instrument used to borrow funds against an asset such as a house. The asset is used as security. If the borrowed funds are not repaid as promised, the lender can foreclose against the asset and use the sale proceeds to recover the unpaid balance of the loan.

mortgage-backed securities: Securities issued for the financing of large pools of mortgages. The promised returns to the security holders are derived from the mortgage interest payments.

mortgage default rate: The percentage of home mortgages on which the borrower is ninety days or more late with the payments on the loan or it is in the foreclosure process. This rate is sometimes referred to as the serious delinquency rate.

mutual funds: An entity that pools the funds of investors and channels them into various categories of investments. There are a variety of mutual funds, including equity funds, bond funds, real estate funds, and money-market funds.

national debt: The sum of the indebtedness of a government in the form of outstanding interest-earning bonds. It reflects the cumulative impact of budget deficits and surpluses.

national income: The total income earned by the citizens of a country during a specific period.

nominal return: The return on an asset in monetary terms. Unlike the real return, it makes no allowance for changes in the general level of prices (inflation).

occupational licensing: A requirement that a person obtain permission from the government in order to perform certain business activities or work in certain occupations.

open markets: Markets that suppliers can enter without obtaining permission from governmental authorities.

opportunity cost: The highest valued alternative good or activity that must be sacrificed as a result of choosing an option.

personal income: The total income received by domestic households and noncorporate businesses.

physical capital: human-made resources (such as tools, equipment, and structures) used to produce other goods and services. They enhance our ability to produce in the future.

plunder: The act of acquiring things by taking them from others.

pork-barrel legislation: Government spending projects that benefit local areas but are paid for by taxpayers at large. The projects typically have costs that exceed benefits; the residents of the district getting the benefits want these projects because they don't have to pay much of the costs.

portfolio: The holdings of savings, investments, and real assets such as real estate owned by an individual or financial institution.

price ceiling: A government-established maximum price that sellers may charge for a good or resource.

price controls: Prices that are imposed by the government. The prices may be set either above or below the level that would be established by markets.

price floor: A government-established minimum price that buyers must pay for a good or resource.

principal: The amount of funds borrowed. The borrower will pay interest on this amount.

private investment: The flow of private-sector expenditures on durable assets (fixed investment) plus the addition to inventories (inventory investment) during a period. These expenditures enhance our ability to provide consumer benefits in the future.

private property rights: Property rights that are exclusively held by an owner, or group of owners, and can be transferred to others at the owner's discretion.

productive function (of government): Government provision of (1) a legal and monetary environment for the smooth operation of markets; and (2) a few goods that are difficult to provide through markets.

productivity: The average output produced per worker during a specific time period, usually measured as output per hour worked.

profit: Revenues that exceed the cost of production. The cost includes the opportunity cost of all resources involved in the production process, including those owned by the firm. Profit results only when the value of the good or service produced is greater than the cost of the resources required for its production.

protective function (of government): A system of rules and laws that protect individuals and their property from damages associated with the use of force, fraud, or theft.

public choice analysis: The study of decision-making as it affects the formation and operation of collective organizations such as governments. In general the principles and methodology of economics are applied to political science topics.

public goods: Goods with the following two characteristics: (1) jointness in consumption—provision of the good to one party simultaneously makes it available to others; and (2) nonexcludability—it is difficult or virtually impossible to exclude nonpaying customers.

random walk theory: The theory that current stock prices already reflect all known information about the future. Therefore the future movement of stock prices will be determined by surprise occurrences, which will cause prices to change in an unpredictable or random fashion.

rational ignorance effect: Voter ignorance resulting from the fact that people perceive their individual votes as unlikely to be decisive. Therefore they are rational in having little incentive to seek the information needed to cast an informed vote.

real interest rate: The interest rate adjusted for inflation; it indicates the real cost to the borrower (and yield to the lender) in terms of goods and services.

recession: A downturn in economic activity characterized by declining real gross domestic product (GDP) and rising unemployment. As a rule of thumb, economists define a recession as two consecutive quarters in which there is a decline in real GDP.

rent-seeking: Actions by individuals and interest groups designed to restructure public policy in a manner that will either directly or indirectly redistribute more income to themselves.

resource: An input used to produce economic goods and services. Natural resources, labor, skills, entrepreneurial talent, and capital are examples. Human history is a record of our struggle to transform available, but limited, resources into things that we would like to have (economic goods).

rule of law: The effective understanding that everyone is subject to the same laws, preventing some from enacting laws that they will not have to abide by.

saving: The portion of after-tax income that is not spent on consumption.

scarcity: Condition in which people would like to have more of a good or resource than is freely available from nature. Almost everything we value is scarce.

secondary effects: Consequences of an economic change that are not immediately identifiable but are felt only with the passage of time.

secondary mortgage market: A market in which mortgages originated by a lender are sold to another financial institution. In recent years, the major buyers in this market were Fannie Mae, Freddie Mac, and large investment banks.

shortage: A condition in which the amount of a good offered for sale by producers is less than the amount demanded by buyers because government has imposed a below-equilibrium price.

shortsightedness effect: Misallocation of resources that results because public-sector action is biased (1) in favor of proposals yielding clearly defined current benefits in exchange for difficult-to-identify future costs; and (2) against proposals with clearly identified current costs but yielding less concrete and less obvious future benefits.

Smoot-Hawley tariff: Legislation passed in June 1930 that increased tariff rates by approximately 50 percent. Other countries retaliated and international trade fell sharply. The legislation was a major contributing factor to the Great Depression.

special-interest effect: The bias of the political process toward adoption of programs that provide substantial individual benefits to well-organized interest groups at the expense of small individual costs imposed on the bulk of voters. There is a tendency for such programs to be adopted even when they are inefficient.

special-interest issue: An issue that generates substantial individual benefits to a small organized minority while imposing a small individual cost on many other voters.

Standard and Poor's (S&P) 500 Index: A basket of five hundred stocks that are selected because they are thought to be collectively representative of the stock market as a whole. Over 70 percent of all U.S. stock value is contained in the S&P 500.

stock: Ownership shares of a corporation. Corporations raise funds by issuing stock ownership shares, which entitle the owners to a proportional share of the firm's profits. The stock owners are not liable for the debts of the corporation beyond their initial investment. However, there is no assurance that the owners will receive either their initial investment or any return in the future.

subprime loan: A loan made to a borrower with blemished credit or who provides only limited documentation of his or her income, employment history, and other indicators of credit worthiness. Federal bank regulators consider loans made to borrowers with FICO scores of less than 660 to be subprime. The interest rates on subprime loans are generally higher than for loans to prime credit customers.

subsidy: A government payment or tax credit provided to either the producers or consumers of certain goods. The payments to producers of ethanol, which sum to about $1.50 per gallon, provide an example.

substitutes: Products that serve similar purposes. An increase in the price of one will cause an increase in the demand for the other, and a decline in the price of one will cause a decline in the demand for the other (for example, hamburgers and tacos, butter and margarine, Chevrolets and Fords).

surplus (in a market): A condition in which the amount of a good offered for sale by producers is greater than the amount that buyers will purchase because the government has set the price above the equilibrium.

tariff: A tax levied on goods imported into a country.

TIPS (Treasury Inflation-Protected Securities): Inflation-indexed bonds issued by the U.S. Department of Treasury. These securities adjust both their principal and coupon interest payments upward with the rate of inflation so that their real return is not affected by the change in rate. TIPS have been issued in the United States since January 1997.

trade deficit: The difference in value between a country's imports and exports, when the imports exceed exports.

trade surplus: The difference in value between a country's imports and exports, when the exports exceed imports.

transaction costs: The time, effort, and other resources needed to search out, negotiate, and consummate an exchange of goods or services.

venture capitalist: A financial investor who specializes in making loans to entrepreneurs with promising business ideas. These ideas often have the potential for rapid growth but are usually also very risky and thus do not qualify for commercial bank loans.

Index

About the Authors

James D. Gwartney holds the Gus A. Stavros Eminent Scholar Chair at Florida State University, where he directs the Stavros Center for the Advancement of Free Enterprise and Economic Education. He is the coauthor of *Economics: Private and Public Choice*, (Cengage South-Western Press, 2015), a widely used principles of economics text now in its fifteenth edition. He is also the coauthor of the annual report, *Economic Freedom of the World*, which provides information on the consistency of institutions and policies with economic freedom for more than 150 countries. His publications have appeared in scholarly journals, including the *American Economic Review, Journal of Political Economy, Journal of Economic Education, Southern Economic Journal*, and *Journal of Institutional and Theoretical Economics*. During 1999–2000, he served as Chief Economist of the Joint Economic Committee of the U.S. Congress. He is a past president of the Southern Economic Association and the Association of Private Enterprise Education. His Ph.D. in economics is from the University of Washington.

Richard L. Stroup is Professor Emeritus of economics at both Montana State University and North Carolina State University. His Ph.D.

is from the University of Washington. From 1982 to 1984 he served as director of the Office of Policy Analysis at the U.S. Department of the Interior. Stroup has published and spoken on global warming, land use regulation, archaeology, and about needed environmental policy improvements. His research helped to develop the approach known as free market environmentalism. He is coauthor of a leading economics principles text, *Economics: Private and Public Choice,* now in its fifteenth edition. His book *Eco-nomics: What Everyone Should Know About Economics and the Environment* (Washington: Cato Institute, 2nd edition 2016), was sponsored by the Property and Environment Research Center, of which he is a cofounder.

Dwight R. Lee received his Ph.D. from the University of California, San Diego in 1972. Since that time he has served on the faculty at the University of Colorado, Virginia Tech University, George Mason University, and the University of Georgia where he was the Ramsey Professor of Economics and Private Enterprise from 1985 to 2008. He was the William J. O'Neil Professor of Global Markets and Freedom at Southern Methodist University in Dallas from 2008 to 2014. He is currently a senior fellow at SMU. Professor Lee's research has covered a variety of areas including the economics of the environment and natural resources, the economics of political decision making, public finance, law and economics, and labor economics. During his career Professor Lee has published over 160 articles in academic journals, nearly 300 articles and commentaries in magazines and newspapers, coauthored fourteen books and been the contributing editor of five others. He has lectured at universities and conferences throughout the United States as well as in Europe, Central America, South America, Asia, and Africa. He was president of the Association of Private Enterprise Education in 1994–1995 and president of the Southern Economic Association in 1997–1998.

Tawni H. Ferrarini is the Sam M. Cohodas Professor at Northern

Michigan University. She was the 2015 president of the National Association of Economic Educators, the inaugural recipient of the National Association of Economic Educator's Abbejean Kehler Award and beneficiary of the 2009 Michigan Economic Educator of the Year Award and an NMU Distinguished Faculty Award. Her work for the Council on Economic Education and reputation as a dynamic workshop leader on both the use of technology in the classroom and the integration of economics and American history helped her earn these awards. She was instrumental in helping establish the Council on Economic Education–Japan and consults for the Korea Development Institute in Seoul. Dr. Ferrarini publishes in economic education, technology, and education journals. She earned her doctorate in economics from Washington University, where she studied under the 1993 Nobel Laureate Douglass C. North.

Joseph P. Calhoun is an associate teaching professor and the Assistant Director of the Stavros Center for the Advancement of Free Enterprise and Economic Education at Florida State University. He currently teaches large principles of economics classes with an annual enrollment of over two thousand students. He regularly presents at national teaching conferences about how to effectively use media and technology in the classroom. A strong supporter of study abroad programs, he has taught in England, Italy, and Spain. Dr. Calhoun has received numerous teaching awards including the Undergraduate Teaching Award at FSU. In 2008, he won first place in the Economics Communicators Contest cosponsored by the Association of Private Enterprise Education and the Market Based Management Institute. His doctoral degree is from the University of Georgia.